SCHINDLER'S LISTED

THE SEARCH FOR MY FATHER'S LOST GOLD

The Holocaust: History and Literature, Ethics and Philosophy

Series Editor:
Michael Berenbaum (American Jewish University)

SCHINDLER'S LISTED

THE SEARCH FOR MY FATHER'S LOST GOLD

Mark Biederman
with
Randi Biederman

BOSTON
2019

Library of Congress Cataloging-in-Publication Data

Names: Biederman, Mark, 1961- author. | Biederman, Randi, 1954- author.
Title: Schindler's listed : the search for my father's lost gold / Mark
  Biederman with Randi Biederman.
Description: Boston : Academic Studies Press, 2019. | **Series:** The Holocaust:
  history and literature, ethics and philosophy
Identifiers: LCCN 2018058725 (print) | LCCN 2018059675 (ebook) | ISBN
  9781644690109 (ebook) | ISBN 9781644690086 (hardcover) | ISBN 9781644690093
  (pbk.)
Subjects: LCSH: Biederman, Mark, 1961---Family. | Holocaust, Jewish
  (1939-1945)--Poland. | Jews--Persecutions--Poland.
Classification: LCC DS134.72.B535 (ebook) | LCC DS134.72.B535 A3 2018 (print)
  | DDC 940.53/180922438--dc23
LC record available at https://lccn.loc.gov/2018058725

ISBN 978-1-64469-008-6 (hardback)
ISBN 978-1-64469-009-3 (paperback)
ISBN 978-1-64469-010-9 (ebook PDF)

Book design by Lapiz Digital Services.
Cover design by Ivan Grave.

Published by Academic Studies Press.
28 Montfern Avenue
Brighton, MA 02135, USA
press@academicstudiespress.com
www.academicstudiespress.com

Dedicated to my father, my mother, all of their family members who were murdered by the Nazis, and my wife Randi who in lieu of Hawaii traveled with me to concentration camps and ghettos across Europe.

Contents

Postwar Midtown Lodz

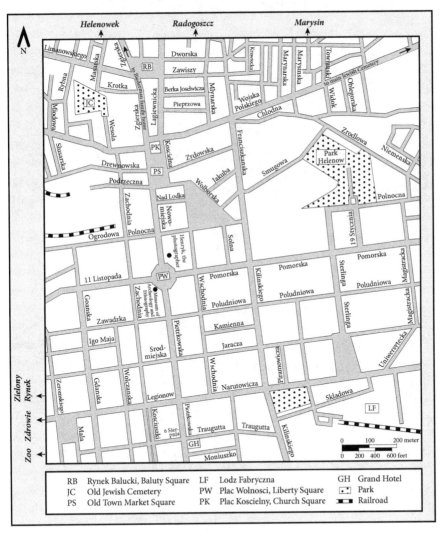

Lodz and Environs during World War II

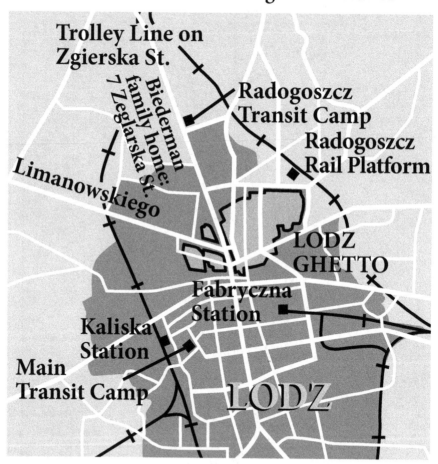

Trolley Line on Zgierska St.

Biederman family home: 7 Zeglarska St.

Radogoszcz Transit Camp

Radogoszcz Rail Platform

Limanowskiego

LODZ GHETTO

Fabryczna Station

Kaliska Station

Main Transit Camp

LODZ

Europe : 1939–1945

- - - - - Harry Biederman's movements
through Europe 1939–1945:

1 Lodz
2 Krosno Airbase
3 Plaszow
4 Gross-Rosen
5 Schindler's Factory: Brunnlitz
6 Mauthausen

Introduction

The most significant event of my life happened well before I was born.

I was born on July 23, 1961 in Detroit, Michigan the son of two Polish-Jewish Holocaust survivors: Harry and Sally (Lipschutz) Biederman. My father was the third person on Schindler's now famous List and my mother came face to face with Dr. Josef Mengele, the infamous Angel of Death at Auschwitz. My parents were deeply scarred by their Holocaust experiences. Consequently, growing up with two parents suffering from post-traumatic stress disorders definitely impacted on me. Neither of my parents slept normally. My mother woke up almost every night screaming, which was audible from my bedroom. My father was a complete insomniac. He would stay up all night and watch television until the networks went off the air and the test patterns came on. For me, it was a boon during the summer school break because I was able to stay up with him through the night and watch TV. World War II movies were our favorite genre. I guess it was somewhat cathartic for him to watch re-enactments of Germans getting killed. On the outside, we may have appeared to have been a normal suburban family, but we were anything but that. Both of my parents suffered from substance abuse. My dad drank heavily, and my mom abused prescription drugs. Somehow, despite his heavy drinking and lack of sleep, my father managed to run a very successful electrical contracting business. Oddly enough, it was a skilled trade that he began acquiring while a concentration camp prisoner.

One of my most vivid memories of my childhood, growing up in the 1960s in Oak Park Michigan, a predominately Jewish suburb of Detroit, was my first neighborhood birthday party. My parents, taking a cue from all the other parents in the neighborhood, hosted a party for my sixth birthday. Right from the start, I noticed that my party was somewhat different from all of my friends' parties. They all had grandparents, aunts, uncles, and cousins in attendance at their party. At my party, the only family members in attendance were my mom, dad, and brother. Naturally, my first question to my parents was: "Where are all MY grandparents, aunts, uncles, and cousins?

Don't they like me?" I remember being shocked by the answer: "You don't have any of those relatives. They were all killed by the Germans."

"What?" I enquired. "Why would anyone do that?" What or who are these awful Germans? I was really ticked off. Grandparents were really nice people and they always gave the best presents! Who would want to kill them? And why?

Shortly thereafter, I was on a trip to the grocery store with my mother when a fateful event occurred: we had finished our purchases and my mother received her change; a few bills and a dime. I had always kept the coins, while my mother kept the bills. On this day, I received a strange dime. It was a 1916 Mercury Head dime. The Mercury Head dime went out of production in 1945 and was replaced by the President Franklin D. Roosevelt Head dime, which was minted shortly after his unexpected death. Occasionally, however, the odd Mercury Head dime could still be found in circulation in the 1960s. I was extremely excited and could not wait for my dad to get home from work to show him my new treasure. After he arrived home, I showed him my new Mercury Head dime and told him I wanted to start a coin collection. I was surprised by his response: "My family had a coin collection once. We buried it in the backyard when the Germans came and threw us out of our home."

Those Germans... again! How can they do that?! Were we at risk of being thrown out of our home? How can that happen?! I needed to find out!

My life's quest had begun. From that day forward, I started reading every book and magazine and watched every movie that I could find related to the Holocaust. I was hoping to find the answers to my questions. Even now, as an adult who has spent his entire life researching the Holocaust, my life in Laguna Beach California is still filled with many unanswered questions. After years of study and travel, I still do not have the all the answers.

My Father's mother and his two eldest sisters.

My father and his youngest sister.

My father's three sisters.

In January 1981, my father died after a protracted struggle with pancreatic cancer. I had just finished my freshman year at Michigan State University. Following my father's death, my mother went into a tailspin. She suffered major bouts of severe depression which led to her being hospitalized. She never fully recovered and over the final thirty-one years of her life she experienced multiple recurrences of depression and was hospitalized repeatedly.

In 1984, my mother was no longer able to take care of the family home

My father and his youngest sister.

My mother's family in downtown Krakow circa 1936; my mother is at the far right with a bow in her hair.

and moved to a condo. While I was helping to empty the house for the move, I began cleaning out my father's nightstand and found three old and faded black and white photos of a boy and three girls. I asked my mother who these people were and why did my dad have these strange pictures in his night stand? She replied that the boy was my father and the three girls were his sisters. I was stunned: I did not know that my father had sisters. What kid doesn't know that his father had three sisters? All these years of Holocaust study and I'd never asked my dad about his own history. I never even knew that he had sisters and I never knew what had happened to them. These three little girls were my aunts, my own family. I was very curious and needed to find out their fate, but was my ability now lost forever?

My first action was to sit my mother down to relate her history before it was also too late. Surprisingly, she produced a similarly old faded photo of her family that I had also never seen before. It is important to note that after the war, neither of my parents had any possessions whatsoever, including family photographs. Fortunately, both of them had relatives overseas to whom family photos were sent prior to the war. My parents were able to retrieve these after settling in the United States. My mother had a first cousin who went to Palestine in 1934 and my father had an uncle who went to Argentina during the 1930s.

Randi and I in the same location in Krakow; August 1996.

My mother was born in Krakow, Poland on November 16, 1924, the middle child of Edward and Felicja Lipschutz. Her older sibling was brother Henryk and she had a much loved little sister, Rena. The family lived in the Jewish quarter of Krakow, named Kazmierz. Shortly after the Nazis invaded Poland, the family was forced to relocate to the newly formed Jewish Ghetto in the run-down section of Krakow known as Podgorze. It was there that Henryk was beaten to death by an SS officer after he stopped during mandatory labor to assist a fallen worker. In March 1942 the Ghetto was liquidated and my mother's family was sent to the Plaszow Concentration Camp on the outskirts of Krakow. My mother and grandmother were selected to work at an electrical factory called Kabelwerke. It was an offsite factory, much like Oscar Schindler's enamelware factory. Her father and sister remained in Plaszow. Her father, Edward had many pre-existing health issues from his service in the Polish Army during the World War I and consequently was in and out of the camp infirmary. During one of Edward's infirmary admissions in 1944, Commandant Amon Goeth, who was portrayed in the movie *Schindler's List*, went through on a routine inspection and ordered all of the patients, including Edward, killed. He was killed by lethal injection of phenol, injected directly into his heart. This was not an uncommon, albeit little known, method of killing prisoners in the concentration camps. After the war, my mother was informed of the details of her father's death by a former neighbor who had been a nurse at the infirmary and witnessed the event. Younger sister Rena, also in 1944, was sent to Auschwitz and was gassed along with all the other children of Plaszow. This was witnessed by another previous Krakow acquaintance who was a *sonderkommando* at Auschwitz. *Sonderkommando* was the term given to Jewish inmates who were selected to work in the gas chambers, removing the dead bodies and transporting them to the incineration pits. They were kept isolated from the general camp population and usually replaced every three months. A select few survived the war. My mother and grandmother went on to survive Plaszow and three other concentration camps.

After interviewing my mother and finding out everything I could about her family, I asked her what she knew about my father's family. She responded that she only knew that they were from Krosno, Poland and had all been killed by the Germans. I told her that I needed to know more. I was determined to find out their stories and what happened to them: including their names, birth dates, and *yahrzeit* (memorial) dates. I felt that it was important for me to know this information, because there was no one else left to remember them. I also asked her if my father had ever mentioned anything about buried coins. She said that my father once told her that he and a friend had gone back to his boyhood home after the war to retrieve some coins buried in their backyard. She said that the house had been occupied by a Polish family and that "the Polak had a gun and shot at them. The friend was killed, and your dad ran away and never went back." Incidences of anti-Jewish pogroms in Poland were rampant after the war. The most notable was the Kielce Pogrom where forty-two Jews returning home from the concentration camps were killed by Polish policemen.

"So the coins are still there?" I asked.

"No way," she responded, and then added: "the Poles dug up every inch of ground when the Jews left. There is nothing there."

"I wouldn't be so sure," I said. "I can't even find my wallet in the drawer where I left it. How are they going to randomly dig up their yards to find something that they don't know is there? Impossible! The coins are still there and I am going to find them, and I'm also going to find out what happened to my dad's entire family."

"How are you going to do that?" she asked.

"Records," I said. "They were from Krosno; certainly I can find an address and birth certificates and go from there."

"Records, shmecords. There are no records…the Germans destroyed everything," she said.

"Nonsense," I said. I knew that in 1942, the Germans decreed at the Wannsee Conference that they were going to find every Jew in Europe and kill them. They kept the minutes of this conference and also intended to document the entire process as proof of their accomplishment for posterity. In order to do this, they needed all the records they could get. Quite the contrary to destroying records, they manically saved them. "The records are there; the coins are there, and I am going to find them," I told my mother.

The Quest Begins

My first step was trying to find a town in Poland called Krosno, which was, according to my mother, my father's hometown and the likely resting place of the coins. This was, by the way, 1984 which was prior to the advent of the internet. There were not a lot of research tools available. In those days, the main resource was the local library. It was there, that I was able to find information about a small town in the southeastern corner of Poland called Krosno, near the Ukraine border. I obtained an address for the city hall and Vital Records Office. I thought this is way too easy! I envisioned simply writing to the clerk, getting my father's birth certificate which, I believed, would include an address for his family's pre-war home. I would then get birth certificates for all his sisters. Being provided with a home address would allow me to just show up in Krosno, dig up the coins, and be on my way.

When I returned home from the library, I enlisted the help of my mother and wrote a letter in Polish to send to the Krosno Vital Records office asking for records of a Biederman family. Three months later, after no response, I sent another pleading for information; I told them that I was doing a genealogy project and I need it completed to graduate from university. After another three months and still no response, I sent another letter and included a ten-dollar bill stating that I hoped it would cover any expenses for the records. After a third three months and again receiving no response, I sent a fourth letter. This time, against my mother's pleading wishes (don't you send those Polaks a dime!) I included a twenty-dollar bill, begging for information. I included a note offering to send more money, if necessary, to secure the records I was seeking. We were now at a year of one-way correspondence. This turned out to not be so easy. Being chastised by my mother was even worse: "I told you—the Germans destroyed all the records. They don't have them and even if they did… they wouldn't give them to you. They HATE you. You are a Jew."

"Mom, how would they know I was Jewish from the letters?" I asked.

"They know! They know a Jewish surname and they have a sixth sense to detect a Jew." She replied.

Finally, I convinced her to write a final letter. This one I sent to the Polish Embassy in Washington DC stating that I needed critical information about my father's family from Krosno, Poland and asked if they could help. At the bottom I said: PS, although my surname is not a Polish name, I am Polish and not a Jew.

I waited for six months and heard nothing back from the Polish Embassy. By now I was a second-year veterinary student at Michigan State University in East Lansing. I decided to take one final shot with the Polish officials. I was in Chicago to attend an MSU vs Northwestern University football game and I was aware that there was a Polish consulate in Chicago. Keep in mind that this was 1985, before the fall of communism. Poland was a tightly controlled communist state. Travel to Poland was not easy. I came up with an idea: I made an appointment to speak to a representative to enquire about getting a visa to travel to Poland. I told the representative that I wanted to visit my father's birthplace but was not sure exactly where it was located in Krosno. I asked if they could help me locate the family's former home. The woman asked me if I still had family in Poland. I responded that I did not. She then asked, "What happened to them?" I told her that my father emigrated from Poland and died in the United States and that the rest of the family had been killed by the Germans during the World War II. Her response was: "Were they Jewish?" At this point, I knew, I was doomed. Needless to say, my visa request was denied and, therefore, my need to obtain information about Krosno was unnecessary, according to the representative. I was told that if I had no living family in Poland, I had no reason to go there.

For the next several years, my research was done in libraries and the Detroit Holocaust Museum. I researched everything about the Holocaust, Krosno, and Polish Jewry trying to find some records of Harry Biederman and family. For the most part, I came up empty although I did learn a lot about the Holocaust and World War II.

Finally, in 1993, five years after graduating from veterinary school, I decided to travel to Poland because I thought if I showed up in person in Krosno, I had a much greater chance of successfully obtaining the information necessary to locate the coins. By this time, communism had collapsed and it was much easier to travel there. After speaking with my mother and many of her survivor friends from Poland, I decided to put the trip on hold. As I recall the advice was something like: "Are you crazy? They will kill you there!" My mother's response was: "You can go after I die because it will kill me if you go there."

1993–1996: Relocating to Windsor

I have never lived a traditional life. Unlike most Jewish boys from Oak Park, I decided to become a veterinarian instead of a doctor, much to the chagrin of my mother. And not just any veterinarian… I went on to become a horse doctor. My father loved to bet on the horses. I assumed it helped him cope with his post-traumatic stress disorders. I grew up around the racetrack and became a racetrack veterinarian. In 1993, the racehorse industry in Michigan collapsed due to the poor economy, so I relocated my veterinary practice to Windsor, Ontario, Canada. I had decided to focus on equine surgery, and since the equine industry was still thriving in Ontario, it seemed like a logical move. Windsor was right across the river from Detroit, so I was still very close to home.

I had kind of reached an impasse on my research. Not that I'd abandoned the quest, I was just focused on launching my new surgical clinic and in those pre-internet days, research was so arduous and time consuming. Since very few of the records were computerized, one had to do an in person search at the site where the archives were stored. Specific searches were conducted by painstaking page by page reading. What, at that time, took several hours or days (and possibly required travel) now is done in milliseconds on a Google search.

I rented a condo in Windsor on Riverside Drive West, across the street from the Holiday Inn, which, interestingly, housed a movie theatre called the Odeon. In early spring 1994, the movie *Schindler's List* opened there. I went to see it multiple times. Little did I know that it would have great significance to me in regards to my father's history. I was drawn to it because it mainly took place in Krakow, Poland which was my mother's birthplace and home town. From what I knew at the time, I saw it as her history and that of her family.

As a result of the movie, *Schindler's List*, there was an explosion of interest in travel to Poland. Jews wanted to travel to see these sites. I wanted to go, too.

In April 1996, I met my future wife, Randi. We talked... a lot. And some of the things we talked about were my family's history, the Holocaust, and the coins. I told her how I had always wanted to go to Poland and she asked: "What are you waiting for... let's do it!" So, as simply as that, we booked a flight to Frankfurt, Germany, arranged for a car rental and were on our way in August 1996. Before we left, we stopped at the local Radio Shack and bought a metal detector: the type you see being used by people on the beach looking for coins in the sand.

1996: Travel to Poland

We flew out of Detroit Metro Airport and settled in for a long flight. We arrived at around 8:00 a.m. local time in Frankfurt, picked up our Opel, and were off. We headed east through the German countryside, through the Fatherland. It was daunting: a jumble of conflicting emotions. I was in the homeland of the people whose goal only fifty years earlier, was to eradicate my people. In spite of my eagerness to see and experience Europe, I wondered, what was I doing here? I pushed the doubts out of my mind and pressed on. I had a purpose, goals, and I was going to accomplish what I had set out to do.

As a student of history, I wanted to see the historic city of Nuremberg. It really was a beautiful place: the medieval castle, the architecture, and the bridges over the Pegnitz River. I, however, was going primarily to see March Field, the Nazi Party rally grounds, and the jewel in the crown of Albert Speer, Hitler's architect and author of the monumental book *Inside the Third Reich*. I had read this book when I was nine years old. It took a while to find March Field. At that time, it was still pre-GPS, and our maps specifically did not mention any Nazi sites. The locals were also not at all helpful in directing us to the spot. Eventually we did find it and, oh, what a sight! It was still so recognizable from the World War II newsreels. The place was virtually abandoned. I got on Adolf's stage and started giving a speech. I imitated Hitler by yelling and flailing my arms and adjusting my hair. I made Randi take pictures. She thought we were going to be arrested. I must say, I enjoyed that.

We then got back in the Opel and headed south to Munich, another beautiful Bavarian city. By now I was feeling the effects of sleep deprivation and jet lag. We checked into a hotel and crashed for a few hours. We awakened at around 2:00 a.m. and just walked around the city center. We saw all the tourist stuff: the Glockenspiel, Fraukirche, and Marienplatz.

The next morning we headed to Dachau. I didn't expect the concentration camp experience to be as light hearted as the initial part of the trip had been thus far. Even the name Dachau sounds so harsh and diabolical. When we arrived at Dachau, however, it surprised me: It didn't appear overtly evil. It was nicely cleaned up and landscaped with tree lined streets. It looked like a rural holiday camp. How could such atrocities have been committed in such a bucolic spot? Obviously, the Germans had gone out of their way to sanitize this place. It was the first concentration camp that we visited and it was deceptively beautified. As we went east, this was less the case. The Poles didn't find it necessary to sanitize the past.

After Dachau, we were off to Salzburg, Austria, childhood home of Mozart. It is a beautiful town with baroque architecture and alpine vistas. It was a nice place to visit but with no historical significance to World War II it was not what I had come to Europe to see.

Next we were off to Linz. I wanted to see Linz for a number of reasons. It was the boyhood home of Adolf Hitler, the location of the displaced persons camp where my parents lived prior to emigrating to the US, and the burial place of my maternal grandmother. My maternal grandmother's name was Felicja Lipschutz. She survived the war, enduring multiple concentration camps only to succumb shortly after liberation. She was buried in the Jewish section of the St. Barbara Friedhof cemetery. It was actually a challenge to find the Jewish section. We arrived and went in through the main entrance. We walked around quite a while and we were not able to find it on our own. I asked one of the landscape staff, in rudimentary German:

Mark at the Nazi parade grounds in Nuremberg.

"Where is the Jewish section?" I was rudely waved away. They were not going to be any help. I think I experienced my first taste of pan-European anti-Semitism. It would only get worse. We went back to the car, a bit dismayed. We were not ready to give up so we re-checked the Linz city map and it showed that the Jewish section was at the back of the cemetery. It was walled off from the Christian part and had a separate entrance. Its entrance was off a deserted street and was sealed with a rusted gate. The Jewish cemetery appeared to be mostly abandoned and untouched since the immediate post-World War II period. We had to climb over the locked gate and wade through hip high weeds. We were able to locate my grandmother's head stone according to its shape from a photo that my mother had given me. The engraving had mostly eroded. We left flowers and continued on our journey.

After a quick stop at Mauthausen Concentration Camp we continued to Vienna and then on through the Czech Republic (where we were stopped by a local police officer and fined twenty dollars for some fictitious infraction) and into the largest Jewish graveyard in the world: Poland. For years I had listened to my parents' tales of the horrors of murder and anti-Semitism of Poland. Crossing the border into Poland was the most difficult thing that I had ever done: it was a daunting prospect to actually, voluntarily cross into that country. There were several times as we drove along that I was tempted to turn around and go back. After much coaxing from Randi, I followed through and entered Poland. After an agonizing wait, we cleared customs. Our first stop was the most infamous place on Earth: Auschwitz-Birkenau. It was here that my mother's younger sister was gassed to death on May 14, 1944. My mother and her mother arrived in July of that same year.

Auschwitz-Birkenau, Poland: July 1944

It was a blistering July day when the train passed through the red brick arch and entered Birkenau Concentration Camp. Inside the airless cattle cars temperatures reached one hundred degrees and the pungent smell of sweat, urine, and feces was asphyxiating. Felicja and Sally were initially relieved when the doors slid open and there was actually tolerable air to breathe. Upon disembarking they were immediately greeted by the Trawniki[1] with their whips, rifle butts, and barking dogs. There was pushing and shoving as the other twenty-seven railway cars which were part of their convoy from Plaszow were opened and the passengers attempted to disembark. Once off the train, Sally and Felicja joined the line of 2,700 Jews being herded towards the rear of the camp.

When they reached the end of the line, Sally and Felicja were standing in front of SS doctor Josef Mengele who was motioning people to the left towards the barracks or right towards the large red brick structure with the huge chimney spewing acrid, black soot. Dr. Mengele motioned for Felicja to join the stream of humanity going right and for Sally, a beautiful red head with piercing blue eyes, to head left. After three steps, Sally jumped out of line, grabbed her mother, and pulled her into the line going left. They were both immediately attacked by the Trawniki, striking them with their weapons. Sally and Felicja were forcibly separated and sent in opposite directions. As soon as the Trawniki stepped away, Sally would again run to grab her mother and take her into the "good" line. When the Trawniki came again to separate them, there was a scuffle which drew the attention of the

---

1   The Trawniki were former Ukrainian prisoners of war who volunteered to be trained by the Germans to serve as concentration camp guards. Their name originated from the town of Trawniki in eastern Poland where they were initially incarcerated. They were known for their particular brand of brutality and were considered to be worse than the SS.

infamous Angel of Death, Dr. Mengele: "What is going on there?" he asked. "We need to keep the line moving!"

A Trawniki guard said: "This fucking Jewess won't let go of her mother."

Mengele came over and was immediately enchanted by this spunky red headed beauty. "How old are you, bitch?" he asked.

"I am nineteen" Sally responded.

"Then you are old enough to be weaned."

"You can shoot me right here, but I am not going one step further without my mother. You already killed my father, brother, and sister."

"Bring her mother here" Mengele told the Ukrainian.

"Can you cook?" Mengele asked of Felicja.

"She's a great cook." Sally piped in.

Mengele paused in thought for a moment, and then said: "Take these two women directly to the camp kitchen and put them to work."

The Ukrainian responded: "Shouldn't we take them for head shaving and tattooing first?"

"Do not touch one hair on her head, just take them right to the kitchen." Mengele replied.

Sally and Felicja had survived the selection.

Being assigned to the kitchen likely saved both of their lives. The inmates assigned to the kitchen were kept separate from the general camp population and were much better fed. They also were exempt from the grueling four-hour daily roll calls in the assembly square. These roll calls were conducted regardless of the weather and proved fatal to many inmates.

Auschwitz-Birkenau: 1996

Appropriately, as we pulled into the Auschwitz parking lot, the skies opened, and a torrential rain ensued. We waited for the storm to subside and finally entered Auschwitz I, the less sinister of the two-camp complex.

Auschwitz I was originally a Polish army barracks and then was used by the Germans as a slave labor camp. Although it had a small gas chamber, it was not a major death factory. It consisted of approximately twenty brick block houses. Many people of different nationalities were incarcerated here—not only Jews; there were also Gypsies, petty criminals, political prisoners, and prisoners of war. Each country which had victims in Auschwitz had a separate memorial in its own block house. The Jewish one was life changing for me. It was an empty dark building that on the inside was designed to resemble a gas chamber. After walking through a dimly lit narrow corridor to reach the basement level, we encountered an illuminated Star of David in an otherwise completely darkened room. The haunting lyrical Hebrew memorial prayer for the dead (Kaddish) was looped through speakers in the background. I was overcome with emotion.

For many years I was critical of Jews who went like sheep to the slaughter even though I was easily intimidated by authority myself. I came out of the block house vowing never to be pushed around again. This vow later came in handy with an encounter with a Polish police officer.

After visiting Auschwitz I, we then drove the short distance to Birkenau which was the actual killing factory. It was here that my mother and grandmother had arrived fifty-two years earlier. Other than the ominous rail gate and guardhouse, most of the original camp structures have been destroyed. Specifically, the four gas chamber/crematoria complexes had been demolished in 1944 by the SS during the German retreat from the advancing Red Army. We walked through a few of the remaining structures and then headed for Krakow, my mother's hometown.

The rain storm passed, and it turned into a beautiful, sunny summer day. We drove in silence, the long hour to Krakow. It was an emotionally complex day. As we turned left into our hotel, we were stopped by a local Polish police officer. Oh no, another Eastern European police shakedown!

As the cop approached the car he showed me a placard which showed a "no left turn" insignia even though the road sign showed left hand turn lane for the Forum Hotel. The cop spoke to me in German and asked for my passport. I assumed he thought I was German because the rental car had German plates. I stepped out of the car and being 6'3" and 260 pounds, I towered over the diminutive Polish cop. He was maybe 5'9."

I told him that I wasn't a fucking German and was not going to give him my passport. "I am an American Jew and you can go fuck yourself," I said in Polish. "You owe me money. You Poles have stolen enough Jewish property. This is one Jew you are not going to rob. Now I am going to park the car and check in. You do what you got to do." The cop was stunned and did not know how to respond. After a few moments of hesitation he mumbled: "Don't do it again" and got in his car and drove off. While I got away with this, my lawyer advised me not to try it again.

I kept my vow that I made in Auschwitz and was a changed man. From that day forward Mark Biederman was never going to be pushed around again.

We proceeded to check into the hotel and asked the concierge about organizing a driver to take us to Krosno. He mentioned that Stephen Spielberg's personal driver during the filming of *Schindler's List* was a cab driver and could be hired for a daily rate. I would not be surprised to hear that fifty guys claimed to be Stephen Spielberg's personal driver, but this

Entrance to Auschwitz-Birkenau.

guy seemed legit. After booking the driver to take us to Krosno the next day, we took a walk around Krakow.

We first visited the old Jewish Quarter of Kazmierz and then went on to Podgorze, the site of the former Jewish ghetto. Along the way, of course, we saw all of my mother's childhood residences. My mother moved several times as a child to increasingly better homes as her father became more successful. He was the owner of a factory that made hats. My mother, like myself, was hypermnesic and could recite all of her previous addresses in Krakow, she gave me a list of them before we left Windsor.

When we returned to our hotel, before retiring for the evening, I took out the metal detector and read the instructions with great anticipation for use in Krosno. I read that the machine had a depth range of one inch maximum. I was devastated. This machine was useless for our purposes. If these coins were still in my father's back yard some fifty-seven years later, they must've been buried much deeper than one inch. I took the unit and disgustedly threw it in the trash bin. Randi asked me: "What are you doing that for?" I replied: "What else am I going to do with this piece of shit?"

The following morning, we met Mishkel, our driver. He gave us an insider tour of the *Schindler's List* sites in Krakow. Most haunting for me was the sight of the balcony of the villa where SS Commandant Amon Goeth randomly shot Jewish prisoners traversing the courtyard, as graphically depicted in the movie.

Schindler's factory in Krakow, August 1996.

At the time we visited, Schindler's factory building was still in use as an electronics manufacturing plant. It became a museum in 2007. Today, there is a copy of the list engraved in the wall of the museum's atrium. Next was the sixty-six-mile trek to Krosno.

When we arrived in Krosno, we were shocked at its blighted state. The town square was an old medieval courtyard with decaying, broken down stone buildings with peeling paint. The entire place reeked of mold. We located the city hall and walked up to the information kiosk. There were two very unpleasant looking women seated at the counter. One appeared to be around sixty years old; the other was probably around thirty-five.

"Good morning," I said. "Didn't you get my letters?" I didn't get a response, just dirty looks. "Can you tell me where I can obtain birth certificates from the pre-World War II era?"

The older woman said to the younger in Polish: "They are Jews, say nothing." She then turned to me and said: "We have no records. Everything was destroyed by the Germans. Go home."

I am thinking: has she been talking to my mother? As we turned to leave, I saw an arrow pointing to the basement down some rickety warped wooden steps that read: "Archives." We followed the sign. Once downstairs, we came upon a table stocked with blank file cards and a sign that instructed us to fill out the last name of the person whose records you are seeking. Behind the table was a glass enclosure. I wrote: "Biederman" on the form and handed it to the clerk through a teller window in the enclosure. She looked at the card, looked at me and then crumpled it up and threw it in the garbage. She then put a "closed" sign up in front of her window. Randi and I looked at each other and I said: "I don't think they like us very much." Randi responded: "We are not going to do well here." Mishkel suggested that we go to the main post office and see if they had any archives or records.

Since we had no success whatsoever at the city hall, I decided to try a softer approach. I went in and chatted up the postal clerk and bought a collection of stamps. I told her I was a collector and that Poland has the most beautiful stamps. I also told her that my father was a proud Pole and loved the country and that he was a native son of Krosno. I went on telling her that he had died when I was young and that my dream had been to visit his childhood home and I was wondering if there were any postal archives or records from the 1930s which I could access.

After taking my money, she handed me the stamps and walked away from the window. I waited for a few minutes hoping she would return with some information for me. She did come back, but proceeded to put a sign on the window:

...Groß-Rosen–A.L.Brünnlitz/Liste d. manl. Häftlinge, Stand 18.4.1945.

d. u.Nat.	H.Art H.Nr.	Name und Vorname	Geburtsdatum	Beruf.
Ju.Po.	68821	Krischer Hirsch	15. 8.97	Autoschlosser
"	2	Vogel Gedale	5. 7.01	Fleischermeister
"	3	Biedermann Hirsch	7. 9.25	Ofensetzerges.
"	4	Weinberger Jachum	16. 5.21	Zimmerer
"	5	Wein Wolf	9. 6.00	Schneidermeister
"	6	Blaemer Jakob	4. 5.15	Bilanzbuchhalter
"	7	Horn Josef	4. 2.14	Schreibkraft
"	8	Klinghofer Simon	25. 3.97	Schneider
"	9	Mahler Abraham	7. 4.02	ang.Metallverarb.
"	68830	Leichter Jocek	25.11.17	ang.Metallverarb.
"	2	Weinschelbaum Dawid	14. 2.24	Monteurgeselle
"	3	Rottenberg Beer	9. 8.20	Elektrikerges.
"	4	Jakubowicz Jakob	13.11.27	Maurerges.
"	5	Weinschelbaum Finkus	24. 9.19	ang.Metallverarb.
"	6	Scheck Jerzy	25.12.17	Maschinenbautechniker
"	7	Weil Naftali	10. 9.14	ang.Metallverarb.
"	8	Gottselig Dawid	6. 5.20	Maurer
"	9	Hornung Josef	6. 9..	Bauingenieur
"	68840	Hornung Dawid	25. 2..	Maschinenbautechniker
"	1	Birnback Ignazy	17. 2.17	Glaser
"	2	Wohlfeiler Ignazy	1.10.95	Glasermeister
"	3	Taube Maksymilian	17. 6.27	ang.Metallverarb.
"	4	Hirschfeld Samuel	27. 2.19	Eisendreher / Fräser
"	5	Taube Emanuel	16. 1.02	ang.Metallverarb.
"	6	Krug Samuel	15.12.11	ang.Metallverarb.
"	7	Schlesinger Moses	5. 7.96	Schlosserges.
"	8	Tennenbaum Izydor	1.10.20	Maurer
"	9	Sperber Chaim	7. 7.03	Schlossergeh.
"	68850	Scheidlinger Markus	19. 8.18	Schlossergeh.
"	1	Horn Eliasz	29. 9.07	Werkzeugmasch.-Fachm.
"	3	Urbach Dawid	18. 2.96	ang.Metallverarb.
"	5	Lamensdorf Leib	14.12.90	ang.Metallverarb.
"	6	Kopyto Moses	14. 3.98	Eisendreher
"	7	Grüss Abraham	6. 9.06	ang.Metallverarb.
"	8	Hirschberg Herz	16. 5.27	Schlossergehilfe
"	9	Segal Chaim	30. 3.07	ang.Mechaniker
"	68860	Schlesinger Abraham	2. 9.10	Schlosser
"	1	Künstlinger Joachim	11.11.15	ang.Metallverarb.
"	2	Oberfeld Adolf	24. 9.11	ang.Metallverarb.
"	3	Schlang Dawid	8. 7.05	Klemnerges.
"	5	Baral Samuel	26.10.04	Stanzer
"	6	Herz Ludwig	19. 9.25	Maler
"	7	Hudes Izak	26. 1.16	Lackierer
"	8	Bleiweiß Efroim	23.12.06	ang.Metallverarb.
"	9	Hellmann Michal Leib	8. 5.22	Zimmerer
"	68870	Manskleid Anatol	15. 5.25	Schlossergehilfe
"	1	Klinghofer Ignacy	30. 1.25	Autoschlosser
"	2	Lewertow Jakob	10.11.08	Stanzer
"	3	Herschlag Abraham	2. 3.20	Schlossergeh.
"	4	Herschlag Salomon	15. 8.22	Schlossergeh.
"	5	Haar David	20.12.12	Klempner
"	60	Zimet Dawid	1. 6.14	ang.Metallverarb.
"	7	Goldschmied Aron	2. 2.23	Schlosserges.
"	8	Klingenholz Aron	18. 6.22	Schlosserges.
"	9	Hosenhaaner Rafal	9.10.00	Buchhalter

The first page of Schindler's List with my father's name highlighted.

"ZAMYKANY" (CLOSED). I quickly realized that we were not likely to get any help from these folks.

Mishkel explained that the Poles feared that Jews were returning to Poland in search of restitution for homes, businesses, and property confiscated during World War II and, therefore, they were reluctant to give out any information that could be used to substantiate a claim. I thought it was just an excuse for good old-fashioned Jew hatred. He suggested we find the old Jewish neighborhood and look for some seniors to see if anyone remembered the Biedermans. We walked around for a few blocks and drew nothing but blank stares. Either none of these people knew the Biedermans or if they did, they wouldn't admit to it. One interesting thing we did see was the ruins of the old Jewish cemetery which, little did I know at the time, contained the remains of my grandmother and two oldest aunts, in a mass grave.

We left Krosno, dejected. We failed in our attempts to determine an address or obtain any official documentation that would substantiate that the Biedermans ever lived in Krosno. I decided that I have to do much more research at home and come back with some concrete evidence, before trying this again. I could not wait to leave this God forsaken place. We departed from Europe, having seen a lot but not really having done what I set out to do.

On one of my first days back at work in Ontario, a horse trainer client and movie buff, Jack Darling, asked me how my trip was and if my father was on Schindler's List. I asked him what would make him think my dad was on the List. He said that while I was away, he bought the VHS tape and noticed when the camera panned the List, a Hirsch Biederman was listed. I

Ruins of the Jewish cemetery in Krosno, which, unbeknownst to me at the time, contained the remains of some of my family members.

told him that I didn't think it was my dad but I would check it out. My father never mentioned anything about Schindler or his List but then again, he died twelve years before the movie came out. I surmised that to him, it was not significant. There were a lot of private industrialists who employed Jewish slave labor. There were a lot of lists.

When I got home, I watched the movie myself and sure enough, in the bonus feature: "The Making of Schindler's List" you could clearly see the name Hirsch Biederman with my father's birth date: September 7, 1925. I was flabbergasted! This was amazing… I now had a list of 1,200 people who possibly knew my father and could potentially provide me with critical information that could help me locate the buried treasure!

Another huge development was occurring almost simultaneously that would change research forever: the Internet became widely available. We bought a dial up modem and signed up for an AOL account. The first search I ever did was: "Schindler's List." Eventually I found a copy on line of the original list and to my surprise, my father, Hirsch Biederman was the third name listed!

The next search I did was for Jewish records in Poland. A brand new site came up: JewishGen.com. It featured the ability for researchers to enter a town in Poland and link with Jewish survivors from that town. I entered Biederman/Krosno and my new email address and waited for a response. A few days later, I got an email from an Albert White in Phoenix asking if my father was the Hirsch Biederman from Lodz, Poland who was with him at the Krosno Airbase. I had no idea about either of these facts but did remember that when watching war movies with my dad as a young boy, he had an uncanny knowledge of German planes. He would name every plane in the scenes: "that is a Stuka, that is a Messerschmitt, that is a Heinkel bomber." I never thought to ask him how he knew so much but amazingly, I think I just found out.

I sent Albert the oldest photo I had of my father which was from 1948 and asked if this was the man he knew. He responded: "Yes, we were in the same barracks together at the airbase." I then sent him a list of questions: How did you know he was from Lodz? How did he get from Lodz to Krosno? Was Albert also on Schindler's List? He answered that my father was definitely from Lodz because they talked about their different childhoods since Albert was a Krosno native. He had no idea how or when he got to Krosno but did know that there were quite a few Lodzers in Krosno. Albert also responded that he was a Schindler Jew but had changed his name from Alex Bialywos to Albert White. Bialy is the Polish word for white.

As I sat reading Albert's latest email I marveled at my amazing luck of finding someone who actually knew my dad during that time. I was especially fortunate to find Albert since I later learned that there were only a handful of Jews who were assigned to the airbase and very few survived the war. My euphoria was short lived, however, as I realized how little I knew about my father and how seemingly hopeless this coin quest has become.

Firstly, was my father from Lodz or Krosno? And more importantly, in which location would his family have buried the coins? I had spent twelve years chasing birth certificates and records in Krosno and now I am not sure and in fact it appears likely that my father was not born there. My heart suddenly dropped into my stomach when I realized the monumental if not impossible task ahead of me. How and where can I find these answers? Countless hours of research lay ahead of me. Was I up for the task?

Around this time, I visited my father's grave in Machpelah Cemetery in Ferndale, Michigan on my yearly pilgrimage on his birthday. I remember saying: "Dad, I'm gonna need your help on this. I am in over my head. Talk to me—where are the coins? What happened to your family?" I then recited a few psalms which I had remembered and also asked God for some help. He owed my dad this, I figured.

Refreshed by my visit, I sat down and wrote out a game plan:

1. I would find out everything I could about the Krosno Airbase;
2. I would find out how Lodz Jews got to Krosno and why;
3. What happened to the Jews of Krosno?

I first posed these questions to Albert White.

He answered that he met my father at the airbase after the Krosno Ghetto was liquidated and all the Jews had been either killed or sent away. He himself was sent from the ghetto to the airbase and believed that my father was already there working with the camp electrician. He had no idea how and when my father got from Lodz to Krosno, nor what happened to his family. He thought that they were all dead by the time he met my father. Albert did say, however, that he still spoke to a lady currently living in New York who was also a Lodz native whom he had met in Krosno. He promised to speak to her and see if she had any information about my father.

I next questioned my mother and asked her why she thought that my father was from Krosno. She responded in her inimitable way: "Because that's what he told me and that's where he is from." I also questioned a few of his closest Holocaust survivor friends if they knew where my dad was from. The two who actually remembered speaking with him about his birth place

(Yoineh Alter and Shlomo Gitler) both said, "of course, he was a Galicianer." The Galicia is a region in the central part of Eastern Europe and today sits in southeast Poland and the Ukraine. It retained its name from the independent kingdom it had been in 1206. Poles from Galicia considered themselves superior to their northern neighbors. The northern neighbors considered the Galicianers to be snobs. The Galicia region of Poland would include Krosno but not Lodz, which is in the region known as the Warthegau. This didn't help me. Why is it that my mother and my father's friends are convinced that he was from Krosno? Had he been lying to them?

A few days later, I got a call from Albert White with great news: Klara Hirsch, his friend originally from Lodz, now living on Long Island, NY knew my dad quite well; in fact she filled out an affidavit in support of my father's restitution claim against Germany.[2] She told Albert that she was an eye witness to the murder of his mother and two eldest sisters in Krosno after they were separated from his father and youngest sister. Albert said she was going into the hospital for a minor procedure, but she would be glad to speak with me once she got home and recovered. After he gave me her phone number, Albert said to call her in two weeks. I could hardly wait! Up until now the Schindler's List survivors whom I had located either could not provide me with any information or refused to speak with me. I respected their wishes; after all, I could barely get my parents to speak to me about their Holocaust experiences, why would these survivors talk to me, a total stranger? I wrote down a detailed list of questions for Mrs. Hirsch: Did you know my father in Lodz? How did you get from Lodz to Krosno? How did my grandmother and aunts die? What happened to my grandfather and youngest aunt? As I waited for the two weeks to pass, I continued to research Krosno, the airbase, and Lodz.

Finally, at the two-week mark, I called the number that Albert had given me. I was so eager to speak with Klara. The phone rang and was answered by a man who said he was Klara's son. I told him that I was Mark Biederman and that Albert White had arranged for me to speak with Klara. His response was: "Sorry can't help you, dude. This is a Shiva[3] house; my mother died last week." I was crushed.

---

2   After the war, Jews were entitled to seek reparations from Germany as a condition of the surrender document. Using a complex formula, they were paid a monthly pension according to days of slave labor, permanent physical ailments suffered, and mental duress. They had to submit documents detailing their camp experience, medical exams and lists of murdered family members. On average, they received about eight hundred dollars per month. I will be explaining this in detail later in the book.

3   Shiva consists of the period of mourning following the death of a loved one. Most Jews observe a one week period of prayer at the home of the deceased or a close family member.

It was now 1997 and my equine practice had taken off and I was working ten hours a day, six days a week. Also, in August 1997, I married Randi who was my impetus for starting this whole quest. My life was full, and it was difficult to spend a lot of time doing research.

In 1998, Randi and I purchased twenty-five acres of land in Maidstone, Ontario (about twelve miles from Detroit) and built a state of the art equine clinic. We built our house ninety feet away from the clinic on the same farm property. Beside practicing medicine and researching my family's past, I was an avid World War II history buff and joined the Military Book Club. I especially had an interest in the Russian front which was kindled when my father's friend showed me a shoebox full of Russian military medals when I was a child.

Each month I ordered every new Holocaust and Eastern Front book that was released. It was in these books that I stumbled across many significant facts which helped me put together my father's past.

After the disappointment of Klara Hirsch's unfortunate death, the next phase of my research was to find proof of my father's birth and residence in Lodz. I enlisted my mother to find any Holocaust survivors from Lodz among her friends and acquaintances. She agreed to talk to people but added: "What do you want from Lodz, it has nothing to do with your father. It is a terrible place."

For my part, I contacted the Lodzer Society (a worldwide group of Lodz Holocaust survivors) and placed an advertisement in their monthly newsletter requesting any information which a member might have about the Biederman family. I also continued to research the fate of the Jews of Krosno in an effort to corroborate Klara Hirsch's eyewitness testimony regarding the murder of my father's mother and eldest sisters with the historical record.

As I awaited a response to my Lodz inquiries, I kept myself busy in my equine practice and reading. One day I made a remarkable discovery about my father. He was witness to a significant historical event which I am about to describe according to my knowledge of the historical record and speaking to eye witnesses who were at the Krosno Airbase.

Krosno Airbase, Poland: August 27, 1941

Hirsch Biederman lay awake in his bunk at 5:15 a.m. wondering why the reveille had not been sounded at 5:00 a.m. like it always had. In his time at the airbase, the German guards would assemble the Jews on the *appelplatz* every day at 5:00 a.m. like clockwork. After being counted, the prisoners would be given their work assignments for the day. This was the first morning that had not happened. Hirsch wondered if this had anything to do with the Focke-Wulfe Condor airplane, tail number 2600 which landed the previous evening and stood under heavy guard on the tarmac. Soon, a message came over the loud speaker: "Attention, attention: all workers must remain in the barracks. Anyone attempting to leave will be shot immediately." Suddenly, the barracks were surrounded by jack booted SS men in black uniforms with the silver braiding on their left sleeve: "Liebstandarte Adolf Hitler." A few moments later, a black six-wheeled Mercedes Touring car drove up and parked in front of the Focke-Wulfe Condor airplane. Hirsch could witness this all very clearly from peering through the window adjacent to his bunk. From the rear of the Mercedes, a portly figure emerged. He was wearing an unfamiliar black uniform with many military decorations. Hirsch believed that he recognized this man from newsreels at the cinema that he had seen before the war. From the other side of the car, another man emerged: smaller and thinner, with a familiar looking toothbrush moustache, wearing a long green trench coat. Was he dreaming? Were Adolf Hitler and Benito Mussolini really standing just twenty yards from his window? Hirsch watched as Hitler and Mussolini together walked up to the Focke-Wulfe Condor airplane and shook hands with the German pilot; they all boarded the plane, and then it started up and taxied away.

I was reading one of my Military Book Club purchases entitled: *Hitler's Secret Headquarters*, where I came upon the chapter "Krosno." From this chapter, I learned that a site near Krosno had been selected in 1939 by the Germans to build a forward airbase for the planned future attack on the Soviet Union. Hitler himself had planned on directing the invasion from a headquarters near this airbase. In 1939, construction began on the airbase and the headquarters. Jewish slave labor was brought in from all over occupied Poland to assist in the construction. Was this the reason why my father and his family had relocated from Lodz to Krosno: were they transported to become slave laborers? The headquarters for Hitler was basically a giant bomb proof concrete hangar where his personal train would be housed. The train was used throughout the war as a mobile command center. It was a monumental task to build this facility. The hangar is still there to this day and is a marvel to visit. Ironically the hangar was only used once. Hitler spent the night of August 26, 1941 there and departed when he returned from the airbase on August 27. It was never used again in the war effort. Because of the unexpected rapid advance of the German army into the Ukraine, this headquarters was too far from the front to be effective. A new headquarters was built in Vinnitsa, Ukraine; it became the Eastern Front headquarters for Operation Barbarossa. The Krosno Airbase, however, continued to function as a heavy long-range bomber base until 1944 and in fact the first planes that bombed the Soviet Union, which started the war between Germany and the Soviet Union, took off from Krosno. They bombed the Soviet Fleet at Sevastopol. Hitler and Mussolini's use of the airbase on August 27 was for the purpose of flying to the Ukraine to visit the German and Italian troops which made up Army Group South and boost morale as their initial advance into the Ukraine had stalled at the gates of Kiev.

My father never mentioned anything to me about the Krosno airbase or the visit by Hitler and Mussolini. My description comes from personal discussions with Albert White on what he remembered about the day Hitler arrived in Krosno. I was able to determine that my father witnessed this meeting from a sketch he made which I had found after he died. My father was a very talented artist and had a collection of sketches which he'd done in his spare time after the war. Most of them depicted scenes of Nazi soldiers abusing Jewish prisoners. This sketch depicted a short, rotund man with a "Roman" nose in a military uniform with many decorations. I was startled when I saw the official Nazi propaganda photograph of Mussolini and Hitler meeting in Krosno. It was exactly the image that my father had drawn. I had no idea until I read the *Hitler's Secret Headquarters* book and saw the photograph of Hitler and Mussolini in Krosno that my father's sketched image was indeed Mussolini!

Speaking to my mother about these sketches, she told me that one day my father planned on publishing them as a testament to his war time experiences. Ironically, both my father and Adolf Hitler aspired to be professional artists when they were young. Circumstances led them both to abandon their plans and they went in completely different directions.

Fate of My Father's Family

In 1999, I was able to find a blurb online which detailed the fate of Krosno's Jewish population. It was on a website called: "Jewish Records Indexing Poland." Jewish Records Indexing Poland was a groundbreaking project begun in 1995 and continues to this day to computerize vital records of Poland from the mid-nineteenth century all the way through and including the Holocaust. Every day, new information became available. This was the blurb:

> On August 10, 1942, the Jews remaining in the Krosno Ghetto were ordered to appear at the main market. From there they were loaded onto cattle cars and shipped to Belzec Concentration Camp where they were immediately gassed to death upon arrival. Those Jews who remained hidden were later rounded up and taken to the Jewish Cemetery and shot and then buried in a mass grave.

As I read this, I nearly fell off my chair. It brought back memories and a huge revelation. My Bar Mitzvah was arranged by my mother and scheduled for August 10, 1974. My father was an electrical contractor and during the summers he worked from sun up to sun down so he left all the arrangements and planning to my mother. I recalled that when he learned of the date of the Bar Mitzvah, he said: "Of all the days, you had to pick that one?" At that time, I had no idea what his complaint was and I never asked him what was wrong with that particular day. My father was a big fan of horse racing. I figured there must have been a big horse race scheduled for that day that he didn't want to miss.

When the day of my Bar Mitzvah rolled around, I was ready. We all got dressed in our Shabbos finest and made the trek to B'nai David Congregation in Southfield, Michigan. I was excited but I still remember that my dad, for some unknown reason, was agitated and in a horrible mood. Aside from that, the Bar Mitzvah went well and I thought my reading of the weekly Torah portion went well.

Later, that evening, we went to the Raleigh House Restaurant (which, as an aside, became famous a year later when it was initially purported to be the location where Jimmy Hoffa's remains were deposited in a dumpster), also in Southfield for the reception. By this time, my dad was completely inebriated. He was uncharacteristically silent with me. He sometimes was that way... he was, after all a Holocaust Survivor and even at thirteen years old, I understood what that meant. He had days that we knew it was best to leave him alone, no questions asked.

After the party, my dad was so distracted that he pulled out of the parking lot and turned left onto Telegraph Road into oncoming traffic: he was on the wrong side of the divided six lane highway! We all screamed thinking we were going to die: headlights were coming at us! Fortunately, he was able to make a quick U-turn and soon we were on our way home. For twenty-five years, I never gave that day and my father's foul mood and behavior a second thought. And now, eighteen years after my father's death, I finally, amazingly, realized what was troubling him on that day. It was the thirty-second anniversary of the murder of his entire family and he did not even mention it! It was obvious that my father did not want his *tzouris* (troubles) to become mine, especially on the day of my Bar Mitzvah.

Going back to Mrs. Hirsch's testimony, I was able to piece together the likely sequence of events of August 10, 1942. It seems that my grandfather and youngest aunt went to the market as ordered, however, my grandmother and two eldest aunts decided to remain hidden in the Ghetto. This would fall in line with my father's own tradition of splitting the family up whenever we travelled. My parents always took separate airplanes and split my brother and I between them. My father felt that flying was dangerous and wanted to ensure that someone survived in the event of a disaster. It seems he learned this from the decisions that his family traditionally made. It remains the custom of observant Jews to say a special prayer in the synagogue giving thanks after they safely fly over a large body of water.

Unfortunately, the decision to split the family on that August 1942 day did not do them any good. My grandfather and youngest aunt were transported to Belzec and were gassed upon arrival. My grandmother and two eldest aunts were discovered in hiding and were marched to the Jewish cemetery and were shot. This is what Klara Hirsch witnessed. Surviving Jews selected as workers (of whom Klara Hirsch was one) dug the mass grave and then had to cover the executed bodies. Some of the Jews who worked at the airbase may also have been taken to do burial duty. To this day, I don't know if my father was one of them. When pressed, my mother did say that she believed that my father was forced to witness the execution of his mother. This took place a month prior to his seventeenth birthday.

As we trudged through the ruins of that abandoned, overgrown cemetery with destroyed headstones, that day in August 1996, little did I know that my grandmother and aunts were there fifty-four years ago and have remained there to this day.

In my research, I found that Belzec (where my grandfather and youngest aunt were killed) was a particularly sinister place. It was one of only four true "Death Camps." Unlike most other camps, it had no barracks to house Jews because there was not an associated forced labor camp at the site. All prisoners brought there were marched directly to the gas chambers. These chambers were supplied by diesel motors which were started after the victims were locked in. They were all slowly asphyxiated by inhalation of carbon monoxide in the fumes of the diesel exhaust. I seethe with anger to this day when I see the picture of my father's youngest sister and imagine what she went through inside this horrible death chamber. Other than two escapees who fled from an arriving train and never entered the camp, there were no survivors of Belzec. It is the only camp with this distinction.

In any event, as disturbing as the facts were, I had achieved one of my initial goals of 1984: I now had the *yahrzeit* date of my father's family. The Hebrew calendar date was the twenty-seventh of Av, 5702.

I Receive Unexpected News

With the discovery of the fate of my father's family, I was beginning to feel that maybe, this was as far as I was going to get in my quest. For the longest time, I was unable to find any information that would link my father to Lodz. I received no responses from the Lodzer Society and although I had met some Lodz Jews, none of them knew any of the Biedermans.

A fateful phone call then came from my mother. As previously mentioned, I attempted to enlist my mother's assistance in locating survivors who may have known my father before the war. I was particularly interested in natives of Lodz because after speaking to Albert White, I was under the impression that my father may have been a native Lodzer himself.

It was March 2001, my mother had just returned from a winter vacation to Florida when she called and asked, "Mark, do you remember Izzy Oliwek?"

"I knew Stan Oliwek, the plumber." I replied.

"Izzy is his brother. I ran into him at the Rascal House Restaurant in Florida. Did you know he was from Lodz?"

"I didn't even know him, how would I have known he was from Lodz? How did you know he was from Lodz?" I asked

"When I saw him, he was reading the Lodzer Society monthly bulletin. So I asked him: 'Are you from Lodz?' He said, 'Yes. What does it matter?' I told Izzy my son is doing a study about his father's family and for some reason, he thinks they are from Lodz." Izzy said that he knew your dad and you should call him.

She gave me his phone number in Florida and I could hardly wait to hear what he had to say.

I called the number and Izzy Oliwek answered the phone. I said, "Izzy, are you from Lodz?"

He answered, "Yes, I am. Why do you ask?"

I asked him: "Did you know my dad in Lodz?"

"Yes," he replied, impatiently. He sounded like he was not well. His breathing sounded labored.

"Did you know where he lived in Lodz?" I asked.

"Yes," he said. The conversation was not flowing so smoothly.

"You would not happen to have his address, by any chance?" I asked rather sarcastically.

"Zeglarska 7," he said.

I didn't even know what to say. I was stunned. I spent seventeen years trying to find out this information and just like that, it got handed to me... By someone whom I did not even know existed. It took me a while to regain my composure. I couldn't even speak.

When I was finally able to gather myself and get some words out, I asked: "How do you know this?"

He replied, "My address was Zeglarska 9, we were neighbors."

I was so shocked that I could not think of any of the thousands of other questions that I had. I just thanked him for speaking to me and hung up.

I jumped in the car and drove to Chapters bookstore in Devonshire Mall in Windsor. I wanted to buy a map of Lodz, Poland to look up Zeglarska Street. They didn't have one but suggested that I go to the Barnes and Noble bookstore in Birmingham, Michigan where they had a huge selection of European city maps. I got in the car and drove across the US/Canadian border via the Windsor-Detroit Tunnel and then raced up the I-75 freeway to Birmingham. Barnes and Noble had a map of Lodz! I bought it, turned around, and went right home with it.

When I arrived home, I quickly unfolded the map and was able to locate Zeglarska Street. It was still there. I was surprised: many streets were eliminated due to post-war reconstruction and many other street names had been changed. I immediately told Randi: "How fast can you pack? We're going to Poland."

As I look back on this today, I wonder: Why did my father mislead my mother and all of his friends into believing that he was from Krosno? Was he so psychologically damaged from the Holocaust that in order to cope, he completely erased his pre-war life in Lodz from his memory? Was the pain of loss too much to bear? Is this how the mind defends itself from insanity? Or was something else going on? I know he had been beaten regularly by the German task masters: was he brain damaged? Did he have memory loss? Or was he guarding some kind of secret? Did he not trust anyone enough to let them know about his past in Lodz? It bothers me to this day: how well did I know my father at all? He died when I was nineteen; was I so wrapped up in my own life that I didn't see what was going on in his?

Another thing that got me thinking: What are the odds of the chance meeting between my mother and Izzy in Florida and would she even have talked to him had he not been reading the Lodzer Bulletin? I had never met anyone before who knew my dad in Lodz and I have not met anyone since.

I have since learned that Zeglarska Street was not in the Jewish neighborhood of Lodz and it is likely that my father and the Oliwek family were the only Jews there. Without speaking to Izzy, there was no other way I could have ever known the Zeglarska 7 address.

Another interesting point is that Steve Oliwek, Izzy's older brother was a plumber and in the summers working for my dad, I would often see him on the same job sites. Steve and my father barely acknowledged each other. I would never have believed that they had been neighbors. Was this part of him erasing his past? Or had something bad happened between them?

Steve Oliwek died in 1991 and Izzy died in January 2002, shortly after I spoke to him. I wish that I would have taken the opportunity to have spoken to him again. There could have been so many questions about my dad and his family that he could have answered. The family that I have never known.

Maidstone, Ontario:
Spring 2001

With the euphoria of learning the location of my father's boyhood home, we began planning another trip to Poland. My excitement was somewhat tempered when I realized that I still did not know for certain that the coins were in Lodz. I didn't know how and when my father's family got to Krosno. From the book about Hitler's headquarters, I knew that some Jews were deported to Krosno but I had no concrete evidence that my father's family was among them.

In September 1939, after Germany defeated Poland in twenty-six days, their forces occupied the western half of the country. The Soviet Union occupied the eastern half of Poland as previously agreed on by the terms of the Molotov-Ribbentrop Soviet-German Non-Aggression Pact of August 1939.

Shortly afterwards, in October, the Germans divided their portion of Poland into two sections. The northwestern portion, which included the Warthegau Province, where Lodz was located, was annexed and became part of Greater Germany. The southeastern portion was renamed the General Government and was placed under the leadership of the Austrian Nazi lawyer, Hans Frank. The General Government was to be a depository for Jews, Poles, and other undesirables, not worthy of German citizenship. The initial solution to the Jewish Question in the newly annexed region, now Greater Germany, was to deport all of those Jews living there to the General Government where they could be exploited for use as forced labor. In the General Government, the Germans were building a military-industrial complex in preparation for the upcoming attack on the Soviet Union. The initial deportations began in December 1939.

Operating on a hunch that my father's family was among the initial deportees, I entered a search at the archives of the Detroit Holocaust Museum: "Deportation List: Lodz to Krosno." Stunningly, I found a list entitled: "List of Jews Deported from Lodz to Krosno." It was in alphabetical order. Under the "B's" there it was: Biederman—Leopold, Esther, Hirsch, Sara, Zilia. One of the sisters' names was missing but I was not surprised. Often I have found that this type of information is incomplete. In the massive undertaking of converting all these millions of documents to computerized files, many transcription mistakes were made, often to the detriment of researchers.

With the discovery of the deportation list, I could now put together a solid timeline of my father's wartime history. Hirsch Biederman was born September 7, 1925. On his fourteenth birthday, the Nazis marched into Lodz. Soon after, anti-Jewish legislation was enacted. Three months later, Hirsch and his family were in the initial group of deportees from Lodz. They were sent to Krosno. According to Albert White, sometime thereafter, Hirsch began working as an electrician's apprentice at the Krosno Airbase. The rest of the family, his mother, father, and three older sisters were confined to the Krosno Ghetto. In August of 1942, the Krosno Ghetto was liquidated, and my father's entire family was killed. My father continued to work at the airbase until it was evacuated in 1944 as the Soviets advanced westward. From the airbase, my father was taken to Plaszow Concentration Camp in Krakow. While there, he was selected to work in Oscar Schindler's factory, where he remained and survived the rest of the war.

From what I had learned, thus far, the coins were either buried at Zeglarska 7 in Lodz or taken to Krosno and buried at some unknown location. At this point I was not ready to definitely commit that the coins were in Lodz.

With this newly discovered information, Randi and I planned our trip to Poland. We were going to visit Lodz for the first time and go to the Zeglarska 7 location and see what the property looked like and to see if the original structures were still there. It was my hope that everything remained the same in its pre-war state. If we arrived and there was a new apartment complex on the site, I would know that, if the coins had been buried there, they were long gone. We also planned to stop in Krosno and visit the site of the former Jewish Ghetto and see if I could find out where my father's family had lived. My mother still insisted that my father had returned to Krosno after the war, not Lodz. If indeed, the coins were buried in Krosno; my odds of finding them were slim.

We booked our flights for mid-June and researched hotels to stay in Lodz and Krosno. When we opened the travel guide, to the Lodz section, it started with: "Mention Lodz to any native Pole and you are sure to elicit a cringe." Our excitement was a little dampened after reading this. We ended up selecting hotels in Lodz and Krosno; we also planned on doing some sightseeing as well as returning to my grandmother's grave in Linz. I had a marble plaque engraved to put on her worn headstone.

New Information Changes Our Course

A few weeks before our departure, we went to Devonshire Mall to shop for things to wear on the trip. As was my habit, I had to go into the Chapters bookstore to check for new World War II history releases. I never walk past a bookstore! There were no new releases, so I selected a few European travel guides. On the way to the cashier, I walked past the discount book rack. On that rack, a title caught my attention: *The Trial of Adolf Eichmann*. I grabbed the three-dollar book and paid for it along with the travel guides.

Adolf Eichmann was a Nazi SS Lieutenant Colonel and one of the major architects of the Holocaust. He was responsible for facilitating the mass deportation of Jews to extermination camps. After the war, he fled to Argentina. In 1960, Eichmann was captured by the Mossad, Israel's famed intelligence/espionage service. After a trial in Israel that was followed around the world, Eichmann was found guilty of war crimes and was hanged in June 1962. He was cremated, and his ashes were scattered in the Mediterranean Sea.

While reading the book, I came up with a startling revelation about my family's coin collection. Eichmann claimed, in his defense that he never ordered the round up or murder of Jews. That was done, he claimed, by his superiors. His job merely entailed scheduling the trains used in transporting people whom others had ordered rounded up and relocated.

In order to rebut this, the prosecution produced an order that was dated December 4, 1939 and was sent to selected Jewish residents of Lodz.

The following dramatization is based on my knowledge of historical events and interviewing eye witnesses and victims of deportations and round ups. It is unfortunate that my father rarely said anything about his experiences during the Holocaust.

December 4, 1939: Zeglarska 7, Lodz, Poland

The tranquility of the quiet Monday afternoon was broken by the black BMW sedan that squealed to a stop in front of the house. It was very unusual to have any cars on the street. This looked to be a particularly ominous vehicle. Hirsch shuttered as he peered out the window and saw the Gestapo man exit the vehicle accompanied by the Polish SS policeman. As they came up the walkway, Leopold, Hirsch's dad, hurried to intercept them at the door hoping to keep them from entering the home.

The Gestapo officer asked: "Are you Leopold Biederman?"

"Yes," replied Leopold.

"This is for you," the officer growled, as he shoved an envelope into his face. "You better read this because we will be back tomorrow." With that, they turned, walked back to their vehicle, and drove away, once again squealing the tires as they left.

"Who was that?" Esther, Hirsch's mother enquired.

"The Gestapo. They gave me this letter."

Leopold, still shaking, sat at the kitchen table, surrounded by his family and opened the envelope. It read:

Attention:

You are ordered to appear with your entire family on December 5, 1939 at the Central Square (Plac Wolnoscie) at 10:00 a.m. for relocation. Each person may bring one small suitcase weighing no more than ten kilograms and each family may bring a total of three hundred zlotys in currency. Failure to comply with this order is punishable by death.

It is so ordered,

Adolf Eichmann, SS Hauptsturmfuhrer, Office of Jewish Affairs

It felt like the air had just been sucked out of the room. No one could breathe, no one spoke.

Then Hirsch solemnly asked: "Father, what does this mean?"

"It means we are getting kicked out of our home."

Hirsch's sisters began quietly crying: "Tata, what are we going to do? How are we going to live? Where are we going?"

Leopold had no answers. Esther, meanwhile, said: "Well, Lodz hasn't exactly been the Garden of Eden. Let's start packing. Come on girls, we will sort through our things and decide what to bring."

Leopold and Hirsch sat downstairs looking at each other. "Tata, what about the coin collection?"

Leopold pondered: "We can't take the coins with us… they are likely to search us and if they find them we will be shot. Plus, they are too heavy and too valuable. They well exceed the three-hundred-zloty limit. There is no way I am just going to leave them for the Nazi bastards. "Hirsch, we are going to bury them in the backyard."

Esther, overhearing the conversation said: "What about the dishes? My pots and pans? The silverware? The candlesticks?"

"We will have to leave them, Esther. We haven't any choice."

"What about packing some food?"

"They didn't say anything about packing food. They had to have made some arrangements to feed us. They can't just let us starve, can they?"

With that, Hirsch pulled out the white ceramic teapot containing the coin collection from its hiding place under the kitchen sink. At midnight, Hirsch and Leopold slipped into the backyard. They surveyed the yard and tried to determine the best spot to bury the coins; not only to obscure them from the view of pedestrians in the street but also to find a spot where the coins could be easily located upon the family's return home. They settled on a secluded spot under the big oak tree next to the alley behind the house. On their hands and knees they dug, using hand spades, to open a one-meter deep hole through the partially frozen ground. They had to work quickly and quietly knowing that they were out past dark and the new curfew was in effect. If a patrol came by and spotted them, they would be shot. Even as they dug, Hirsch could hear the Alsatian dogs barking in the distance. The patrol was getting nearer. They hurriedly placed the pot in the hole and covered their treasure with soil.

Leopold said: "Now Hirsch, are you going to remember where these are?"

They returned to the house and cleaned up. They still had to pack. It was a long night.

The following morning the family quickly ate their breakfast. They dressed heavily, layering as much clothing as possible, grabbed their small bundles and walked out the door for the last time. They began the forty-five-minute walk down Zgierska Street, the main thoroughfare in Lodz to the Plac Wolnoscie.

When they arrived, they were quickly joined by the 2,500 other Jews who received the same notice to appear. Someone asked: "Does anyone know where we are going?" Another man answered: "My neighbor has a friend who works for the Jewish Council. Does anyone have any friends or family in Krosno?"

After reading the order of Eichmann, I came to a startling conclusion: the coins are in Lodz! There was no way that the family would have risked taking the coin collection with them and even if they managed to sneak a few coins to Krosno, they would have surely traded them for food or used them as bribes to survive on a daily basis. Their initial three hundred zlotys were likely gone in a month and they somehow had to survive in Krosno for three more years. The Jewish slave laborers of the General Government received no money and were barely fed. It is impossible that there would have been any money left for my father to unearth in Krosno.

In regards to Eichmann; German officers in the early years of the euphoria of military victories took no efforts to conceal their complicity in war crimes. As the war turned against them, however, they learned not to sign or put in print anything that could be used as evidence of their crimes. This document was one of the few, in print, that Eichmann signed which specifically ordered the deportation and threatened the death of Jews.

At the end of the trial, it was clear that Eichmann not only was complicit, but was the highest-ranking SS officer responsible for issuing the orders for rounding up and exterminating Jews.

Today, it is widely agreed on that Eichmann had a considerable amount of independence and is considered one of the main conspirators in the murder of six million Jews.

After I finished this book, I cancelled the hotel reservations in Krosno. No Jewish Biederman will ever be hassled in that desolate Polish outpost again. From now on, there would be no need to deal with Krosno again. The focus of our search was now to be centered on Lodz. Our flight was scheduled for June 17, 2001. We landed in Frankfurt on Monday morning, June 18 and picked up our rental car. Since our last trip, GPS navigation had become available in Western Europe and we opted for it: it was a big bonus. It was our first time using it and it was great! Unfortunately, we were only able to use it in Germany and Austria. Once we were in Eastern Europe, it was nonfunctional.

Europe: 2001

Although we were primarily in Europe to reconnoiter the family home in Lodz, we also wanted to see some historic World War II sites that we had missed during our first trip in 1996. Our first stop was Berchtesgaden, the site of Adolf Hitler's home known as the Berghof and also the famed Eagle's Nest in the Bavarian Alps. We made a reservation to stay at the Hotel Zum Turken which was a short walk from the Berghof and had its own peculiar history.

The Zum Turken was built in 1911 as a hotel and remained that way until 1933. After Hitler bought the Berghof, which was next door, the SS forced the owner to sell the hotel. Originally, he refused but changed his mind after spending a month in Dachau. During the war, the hotel was used to station SS troops who were part of Hitler's elite personal body guard. The SS guard post is still there at the street entrance. After the war, the daughter of the original owner was able to reclaim the hotel and it has remained in the family and has been in operation as a hotel ever since.

When we arrived, we requested the executive suite. We were given a four-inch long vintage skeleton key with a wooden knob handle. As I accepted the key, I began to think, who else might have used this key? What high party SS officials would have visited the Fuhrer and stayed in this suite? Himmler? Heydrich? Whose DNA was embedded in the wooden handle? It was very creepy.

When we got to the suite, it had an ancient wood framed double bed, likely there since 1911. If I thought the key was eerie, sleeping in the bed was downright macabre. I wondered how many of the SS were rolling in their graves at the thought of a Jew sleeping in that bed.

Aside from the daunting history, the hotel was in a beautiful spot and offered amazing alpine vistas.

For our next stop, we took the short walk to the Berghof. The Berghof was heavily bombed in 1945 by the Allies because it was believed that the Nazis were going to make a last stand in Berchtesgaden and Hitler may have been holed up there. In 1956, what was left of the Berghof was completely razed. The new German government didn't want any remaining shrines to Hitler.

Although only the ruins of the house remained, the cobblestone balcony remained intact. It was from this balcony that many home movies were made of Hitler, Eva Braun and his prized Alsatians: Blondie and her puppies. These have been shown many times on television history shows. It was very recognizable and again, felt very unnerving for me to be standing there.

The following day, we were up at 5:00 a.m. and after eating breakfast, took the walk to the entrance to the Eagle's Nest. The Eagle's Nest was a small stone social hall built atop Mount Kehlstein by Martin Bormann as a fiftieth birthday gift for Adolf Hitler. It was 6,000 feet above sea level and was only accessible by an elevator cut into the mountain. It was used by the Nazis for special occasions. Hitler himself was afraid of heights and rarely visited. The most notable exception is when he and Benito Mussolini met there shortly after its completion.

When we got there, it was not yet open, however, a private tour guide and her Japanese tour group were there. She was about six-feet tall, spoke English with a Bavarian accent and was approximately sixty-five years old. She told us that the Eagle's Nest didn't open for another hour, but she had access and we could join her group. We gladly accepted and got in her bus for the ride up to the elevator entrance. The bus took a nerve wracking, tortuous route up hairpin turns to the 5,500 feet level and parked at the elevator entrance. From there, we took the elevator to the summit. The views from the Eagle's Nest were awe inspiring. The building itself was a marvel of engineering.

As the tour guide was showing the group around, she began waxing nostalgic for the Nazi era, praising the glory days of the Fuhrer. One of the Japanese tourists was videotaping her presentation, and once she noticed him, she erupted: "Are you filming me? I forbid it! You put your camera away." He was stunned and immediately followed her instructions. The camera was quickly tucked away. The guide, thinking that I, at 6'3" with blond hair and blue eyed would be sympathetic, said to me: "You know, there are groups that complain when I talk about the Fuhrer. I have to be careful what I say and I don't allow myself to be filmed."

Randi was completely unnerved and wanted to leave. I convinced her to continue the tour of the Eagle's Nest on our own, because by now, many tourists were arriving as it had officially opened. As we entered the main hall, there were numerous photos of the Nazi era. One of them showed Hitler sitting on a bench with a little Aryan girl on his lap. Was this our tour guide? To this day we still chuckle when we recall the events of the Eagle's Nest visit.

We checked out of the Zum Turken later that day and made the short drive to Linz, Austria. Our next stop was the St. Barbara Friedhof cemetery to visit the grave of my maternal grandmother, Felicja. We brought the engraved marble plaque and special silicon adhesive to attach it to her worn headstone. The plaque was engraved: "Felicja Lipschutz, Holocaust Survivor." It was gratifying to know that future generations would be able to locate her grave.

From Linz, we continued to Vienna, where we stayed one night. After one day in Vienna, we drove to Budapest. My mother insisted that we tour the city because she thought it was so beautiful. I wasn't too impressed, but we did do a night Danube River cruise which was nice. We stayed only one night.

Next we made a big push northeast, through Hungary, into Slovakia and across the Dukla Pass into Poland. The Dukla Pass was interesting for me as an Eastern Front history buff because it was the site of a large tank battle between the Soviet and German forces.

In the summer of 1944, the Slovaks rebelled against the German occupation and asked the Soviets for help in defeating the Germans. The Soviets planned on dashing across Poland, westward into Germany but some of their forces were detoured south to eliminate the threat to their flanks

My grandmother's grave with the new plaque attached.

posed by the Germans forces in Slovakia and to aid the Slovak uprising. The Germans heavily defended the crossing into Slovakia and a huge battle ensued. In the end, the German forces delayed the Soviets long enough to crush the Slovak uprising and Slovakia was not liberated until 1945. At the site of the battle there was a lot of military equipment left behind as a memorial. For me, it was enthralling because it was my first in person view of Russian tanks and planes which I had read a great deal about but had never seen.

We stopped for the night in the Polish resort town of Iwonicz-Zdroj which was highly recommended by Albert White. I don't remember much about the town or why it was considered to be such a desirable resort, but I do remember having pizza for dinner and it was the best pizza I had ever had. Who knew that corn, zucchini, and squash would taste so good on a pizza?

Originally we had planned on going to Belzec to see the site where my grandfather and youngest aunt were killed. We were talked out of it by locals who explained that it was almost impossible to get to due to the lack of highways and paved roads. At that time, they had also mentioned that there was nothing at the site but an empty field. The Germans had demolished the camp in 1943 after having killed the majority of the Jews in the General Government. The few remaining Jews were to be killed at a newer facility in Lublin, called Majdanek Concentration Camp, after they were no longer useful as slave laborers. It wasn't until 2005, four years after this current trip, that memorials were erected at Belzec.

Our next stop was Majdanek. Even though it had no personal connection I wanted to see it because it was purported to be the most intact camp since the end of the war.

Majdanek

Unlike all the other camps, Majdanek is located in the heart of a major city, Lublin. Lublin was, for many centuries, a hub of Jewish learning and boasted one of the largest Yeshivas in the world. It was often dubbed the "Jewish Oxford."

The camp opened in 1941 and was liberated July 22, 1944. It was originally designed as a Soviet prisoner of war camp but was reformatted to become a Jewish extermination camp in September 1942 after the dismantling of the Belzec Death Camp.

If you are going to visit one concentration camp, to get a realistic vision of what they were like while operational, this one should be it. Due to the rapid and unexpected advance of the Soviet Army, the SS did not have the opportunity to dismantle this camp as they had with all the other death camps. Consequently, this is the only camp with intact gas chambers, crematoria, barracks, and other buildings. One of these buildings contained piles of victims' shoes; another had piles of eye glasses, a third was stocked with prosthetic limbs.

At the rear of the camp is a gigantic circular mausoleum which was built as a monument to the murdered victims and consists of a huge open-air urn covered by a dome and holds their ashes and bone fragments. Most disturbing for me was seeing a small scapula (shoulder blade) which was from a young child. I realized that many of my family members suffered this same fate. I had seen enough, I could not wait to get out of there.

Lodz

After touring Majdanek we drove to Warsaw for a short overnight visit and then made the trek to Lodz.

From the travel guides, I was somewhat prepared that Lodz wasn't going to be too pretty. As we approached the city from the highway, it was even worse than I thought it would be. The entire skyline consisted of outdated factory buildings with spewing smoke stacks. It was dreary and the city was enveloped with a brownish haze. As we pulled into the city center, it reminded me very much of Krosno, only much larger. It had the same sort of run down, decrepit appearance.

We located our hotel and checked in. It was an old hotel, named the Grand and it was designed to resemble the grand hotels of Europe. It seemed as if the Poles thought that the name alone would be sufficient. At one time Lodz was a successful industrial town but it had fallen into complete disrepair in the twentieth century. This hotel suffered from the same severe neglect as the rest of the city. Incidentally, after our visit there in 2001, Poland joined the European Union (in 2004) and since then much money has been allocated to modernizing Lodz. The Grand Hotel and the street it is on, Piotrkowska Street (the central street of downtown Lodz) have been updated since our visit. The rest of the city remains virtually the same as it was. The contrast is startling.

By the time we settled in to the hotel, it was after dark so we decided to get some sleep in preparation for the big day tomorrow. We were going to Zeglarska Street, my father's childhood home.

The morning came, and we were off to Zeglarska Street. It was about a twenty-minute drive from the hotel. On the drive, we were taken aback by the tremendous amount of anti-Semitic graffiti. On virtually every wall there was a spray-painted Star of David on the end of a hang man's noose. It was unsettling. There has not been a Jewish presence in Lodz since 1944, and yet the deep-seated anti-Semitic attitude was blatantly obvious. I would imagine that most of the graffiti had been done by young people who have never even met a Jew. I was very tempted to go back to the hotel, grab my bags, and go home.

Zeglarska 7, Lodz; June 2001.

After all, the last time a Biederman showed up to Zeglarska Street, he was shot at. (If the reader will remember, my mother had told me the story about my father and his friend's attempt to retrieve the coins after the war.) In the end, we decided, we had come this far, we had to follow through.

We parked nearby and walked along the narrow cobblestone lane to the house numbered 7. It was a dilapidated two-story concrete building with an untended, overgrown grass lawn. I wondered what could be of value in the yard: the house certainly did not look like the home of someone who would have had a valuable coin collection. Evidently the neighborhood had declined since 1939.

I was very cautious when walking around the perimeter of the house. Maybe the same person who shot at my father still lived there. Randi told me to ring the bell and introduce myself and tell them that my dad lived here as a boy. I responded: "Are you nuts? What am I going to tell him? I am the son of the Jew that lived here before the war. And I'm here to dig up your back yard." We decided it may be best to not announce our presence.

During my surveillance of the house, I noticed that there was a back alley behind the yard and figured that the coins have got to be adjacent to it. I was trying to think what my father and grandfather must have thought as they were seeking a spot to bury the coins. I concluded that they probably thought on their return, they would have to sneak in under cover of darkness to dig them up and the closer to the alley the better.

I did not make this trip to actually attempt to dig up the coins. My goal was to see the property and evaluate whether or not it seemed possible that they could still be buried there. After walking around the property and realizing how untouched in more than fifty years everything appeared, I was convinced: the coins are here. Now, I have to figure out how to retrieve them. I thought perhaps I could buy the property… what could this place be worth? Even then, what? Randomly start digging? I had to go home and rethink the entire venture.

Another photo of the house on Zeglarska Street.

On our way back to the hotel, we continued to notice the anti-Semitic graffiti: it was extensive. It was impossible to go a block without seeing a Star of David on a hangman's scaffold or a "death to Jews" proclamation sprayed on a wall. We had been to Warsaw and Krakow and felt some measure of discomfort, but nothing could have prepared us for what we witnessed here, in this mostly poor, blue collar town. I was beginning to understand the hopelessness and despair that my father's family must have felt in 1939. On the one hand, they had to endure the cruelty of Nazis, invaders of their homeland. On the other hand, they had the local populace, their fellow Poles, many of whom were often equally malevolent towards their Jewish neighbors.

We decided that we'd had enough of Lodz; we went back to our room, packed our bags and checked out a day early. We got in the car and headed for the civility of Germany. Our flight out of Berlin was scheduled in two days: Randi counted the hours until we could board the plane home. Like my father, many years before me, I wasn't sure if I was ever coming back to Poland for these coins or for any other reason.

As we crossed the bridge over the Oder River and into Germany, Randi and I exhaled: it was a sigh of relief. I was reminded of a story that my mother related to me about the time she and my father also left Poland for the last time.

Postwar Europe

My mother and grandmother remained at Auschwitz until October 1944 and then were loaded into box cars and transported to Bergen-Belsen Concentration Camp outside of Hamburg in Northern Germany. By this time, Reichsführer-SS Heinrich Himmler, the leader and chief of the Jewish Extermination Program, had ordered a halt to the gassing of prisoners.

On October 1, 1944, with defeat imminent, he had begun clandestine negotiations with the Allies in an effort to save himself. The first condition that was given to him was to cease the exterminations immediately. Now, instead of being executed, Auschwitz prisoners who were healthy enough to work were being evacuated westward to labor camps deep into Germany, ahead of the approaching Red Army advance. Sick prisoners were simply abandoned and left to starve and die. Dr. Josef Mengele was already planning to flee back to his home, also in Germany. The famous diarist Anne Frank and her sister Margot were also in Auschwitz at this time and were evacuated in the same transport as Sally and Felicja. Ironically, the Nazis had spent eleven years making Germany "Judenrein" (Jew Free) and now in desperate need of labor due to horrific losses on the Eastern Front, they were bringing Jews back into Germany by the train load. A few months after they arrived, as the British advanced on Bergen-Belsen, those prisoners still healthy enough to work were again evacuated. By this time, the Frank sisters had both become ill with typhus and were not healthy enough to be transported; they both died in Bergen-Belsen. Typhus was a common malady in the concentration camps. It is a bacterial infection spread most commonly by lice. It begins with flu-like symptoms, and can progress into a fatal encephalitis in debilitated patients. My mother and grandmother, at this point, managed to stay healthy enough to be selected for transport. They were loaded into box cars and shipped back east, this time to Theresienstadt, just outside of Prague. It was there, in May 1945, that they were liberated by the Red Army. At the time of liberation they also had become very ill and were suffering from typhus.

The Red Army set up a field hospital at Theresienstadt to care for the ill prisoners. My mother always commended the Russian medical personnel for the care that was provided to them. She and my grandmother recovered and left the facility to head back to Krakow to look for other family members who may have survived and to reclaim their home. Survivors were given train passes and freedom of travel throughout Europe for a time.

Upon arrival in Krakow, they immediately went to their former residence in Kazmierz, but were intercepted at the front gate by the custodian. He said to them: "Jesus, Maria, You survived!" He went on to tell them that a Polish family was now living in the home and they would have to leave. Polish courts had ruled that former Jewish property could not be reclaimed. With nowhere else to go, they went to a displaced persons dormitory which was the site of a former Jewish orphanage on Jozefa Dietla Street. This

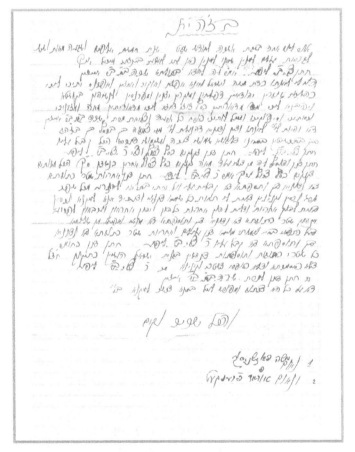

My parent's marriage certificate, handwritten by Rabbi Lewertow.

facility was supported by funds from the American Joint Distribution Committee. At the orphanage, in October 1945, my mother met a man who caught her interest. He was a strong, muscular boy who stood out from the other Jewish men who were hunched over and frail.

When Harry (Hirsch) met Sally, they fell in love at first sight. After just a few months of a courtship, they decided to get married. On January 13, 1946, they were married in a religious ceremony performed by Rabbi Jakob Lewertow who was prominently portrayed in the *Schindler's List* movie and later became the Chief Rabbi of Krakow. Both Sally and Hirsch wanted to raise a family and realized that Poland did not offer a promising future. They decided that they had to get out of Poland so they began planning to head west with the hope of eventually immigrating to America.

In May 1946, they boarded a train headed to Berlin along with Sally's mother, Felicja. They chose Berlin because there were rumors that employment was available there for Jewish refugees. After a long train journey, they arrived in the Soviet sector of Berlin. An announcement came over the loudspeaker: "Please have your documents ready for inspection." Moments later a Soviet border inspector toting a PPSH 41 submachine gun strapped over his shoulder came through the rail car. He went through the train car checking passengers' documents and then waved them off the train with the flick of his machine gun. When he got to my family, he looked at their documents and waved Sally and Felicja off the train. When he looked at Hirsch's documents, however, he blocked his exit and said: "You are a citizen of the People's Republic of Poland and you don't have the proper exit papers." The communist controlled government was not amenable to allowing young, healthy men to leave the country. On the other hand, a frail, unwell Jewish woman and her daughter were more than welcome to go elsewhere. The guard told Hirsch: "You are coming back to Krakow with me." Hirsch yelled to Sally and Felicja in Yiddish: "Keep going, get out of here: don't worry, I'll be back." With those words, Sally and Felicja left the train.

Hirsch and the guard were the last people on the train. Hirsch said to the guard: "What happens now?"

The guard responded: "The train is heading back to Krakow. We are going to wait here for it to depart."

Hearing this, Hirsch reached into his rucksack and pulled out a bottle of vodka and a pack of cigarettes. Hirsch had learned from experience to always travel with a bottle of vodka and a pack of cigarettes. They often got you further than any document ever would. Hirsch opened the vodka and took a swig and offered it to the guard. The guard gladly accepted and took a huge gulp and passed the bottle back to Hirsch. Hirsch put the bottle up to his lips and pretended to take a drink. He then handed the bottle back to the Russian. After half an hour, the bottle was empty. Hirsch produced another bottle of vodka as the train lurched into motion, back toward Poland. The bottle kept passing back and forth: the guard swilling, Hirsch pretending.

Meanwhile, Sally and Felicja went into the train station and found a bench. Sally proclaimed: "I am not leaving here until Hirsch comes back."

Felicja said, "What if he never comes back?"

Sally responded, "Then I will die on this bench waiting for him."

Felicja knew better than to argue with her daughter. So, she made herself as comfortable as possible and fell asleep.

About an hour into the train journey, the guard passed out, completely drunk. As the train was slowing in approach of the Frankfurt an der Oder station, Hirsch, seizing the opportunity, quickly opened the train window and jumped out. He rolled to a stop, uninjured. He then got up, dusted himself off and after orienting himself decided to follow the train tracks back to Berlin. After walking all night, he arrived the following afternoon to the Berlin train station. It took Hirsch a while, but eventually he found Sally and Felicja sleeping on a bench in a quiet corner of the bomb damaged and not yet rebuilt Lehrter Street station. He walked over and tapped Sally on the shoulder: "Let's get out of here," he said.

She was at first a bit startled: who was this mud encrusted, haggard man? She initially did not recognize him. When she completely awoke and realized that it was Hirsch, she was overwhelmed with joy and relief. The reunion was miraculous for them. They immediately headed for the exit and made their way to the American sector of Berlin. It was relatively easy to cross from one sector to the next in 1946.

They checked into the American Joint Distribution Committee hostel in Berlin and exhaled a huge sigh of relief. They were never going back to Poland again!

As Randi and I arrived at our hotel in Berlin, we said the same thing: "We are never going back to Poland again!"

Maidstone, Ontario: 2001 through 2003

When we returned to Canada, one of the emerging issues in equine medicine was the arrival of a deadly foreign zoonotic disease known as West Nile disease. It was a viral disease that originated in Egypt and in recent years had spread throughout Europe. The disease is spread by the bite of an infected mosquito. The mosquito becomes infected when it feeds on an infected bird and then spreads the disease by biting a horse, human or other susceptible species. Of all the veterinary species, the horse is the most seriously affected: mortality rates approach 60 percent in horses. Horses themselves, are not contagious due to a very low viremia (viral levels in the blood). The virus accumulates in their spinal cords and brains. In 2001, West Nile virus had reached the shores of North America: a few cases were discovered in horses in Florida and in the southeastern United States.

For my part, I became alarmed when I began noticing a significant number of dead crows around the farm. Birds are the main reservoir for West Nile virus and when infected, crows suffer the highest rate of mortality. I began to fear that the virus had arrived in Canada. I contacted the Ministry of Agriculture and made them aware of my concerns and informed them of the crow deaths on my farm. I was told that West Nile disease was still a long distance away and the department made no provisions for testing the dead birds. Since affected horses were not able to transmit the disease, there was no travel ban on horses entering Canada from regions where West Nile had been detected, therefore the local Agriculture office, whose job it was to monitor animals entering Canada, was not going to get involved in the matter. In the Standardbred horse industry, there were large numbers of horses being shipped back and forth across the US/Canada border between Ontario and Florida racetracks. As long as there were no restrictions on their movements across the border, nobody really cared about what I had to say about the deaths of a few pesky birds. Fortunately, winter arrived without any horse cases and my fears were eased for the time being.

The following summer, during the annual spike in mosquito population, we had an epidemic of horses afflicted with acute onset of severe neurologic disease. Initially, the horses demonstrated flu like symptoms (fever, nasal and ocular discharge, lethargy, and respiratory difficulty) which progressed rapidly to paralysis and finally death. I had never seen anything like this before. I notified the local Ministry of Agriculture office and told them that I believed we had the initial cases of West Nile disease. They responded that I was inaccurate in my diagnosis and that the West Nile virus had not yet arrived in Canada. I told them I needed these horses to be tested anyway because this disease outbreak was unlike anything that I had previously experienced and I was pretty confident in my diagnosis. They responded that they currently had no ability to perform the test for West Nile virus, nor were there any private labs in Canada which had this capability. I, therefore, called my alma mater, Michigan State University, which was ninety miles away and asked if they had the ability to test for the disease. They told me that they were in the process of developing a test but since they did not have any infected horses, they were unsure of its accuracy. I told them that I had sixteen active cases and could have the serum samples sent to them the next day. The virologists working on the test were very eager to get a hold of serum from possibly afflicted horses and said they would be grateful if I would provide my samples. The following day, the samples were shipped to them. Two days later the results were in; the serum tested positive for antibodies to the West Nile virus, and Canada had its first confirmed cases of West Nile virus disease!

One of the owners of an infected horse contacted the local Windsor media and from there the story spread rapidly. In a very short time, the news spread nationally and then into the United States and I became the go-to media spokesman, throughout the United States and Canada. Needless to say, the publicity and the time devoted to being the newly anointed expert and spokesman for West Nile disease cut into the time I had available to continue my research and planning for the recovery of the family coins and quest to find the names and ages of my father's murdered family. I would spend hours researching the latest developments and statistics of West Nile disease prior to every requested interview. I thought it was important for my reputation to appear knowledgeable. If the media were considering me to be the expert voice on the West Nile situation, I had better sound like one! Humans are also highly susceptible to West Nile virus, so the media coverage was much greater than it would have been had it strictly been a veterinary disease. At least 50 percent of the questions presented to me were concerning human pathophysiology as opposed to any concerns about the horse.

Also in 2002, we began having our first crop of foals born on our farm. Besides practicing veterinary medicine and running an equine surgical hospital, we decided to begin breeding Standardbred racehorses. Randi bought her first racehorse in 1998 and after four years of success, wanted to move into the next level: breeding and raising them. Horses are seasonal breeders and have a relatively short three-month breeding season in the spring, followed the next year by a relatively short foaling season. Their gestation period is close to one year.

The foaling process usually goes smoothly in a horse but when problems do occur, they are very serious and require immediate veterinary attention. For this reason, it is important to constantly monitor any imminent foaling mare. Most horses go into labor and deliver their foals after midnight. We had a closed-circuit video system, with cameras in each horse stall, installed and I watched the monitor all night from the house when we thought a mare was ready to foal. I was awake most of the night during foaling season and therefore had a lot of time on my hands and would alternate between Direct TV and the video monitor. Needless to say, I watched a lot of television. My station of choice was the History Channel, which in their early years primarily showed World War II themed programing.

It was on one of these prospective foaling nights that I watched a show about an organization called "Berliner Unterwelten" (Underground Berlin). The continuing series of shows featured a group of researchers going through Berlin searching for buried former Nazi historical sites. In this particular episode, they were searching for the exact location of Hitler's Fuhrerbunker. The researcher was rolling a device that looked like a lawnmower over a parking lot where the bunker was rumored to be buried. The show host asked him what that device is and what is its purpose? The operator replied that it was called a Ground Penetrating Radar and it could find disturbances in the soil deep within the ground. At this time, he was looking for the exterior walls of Hitler's bunker.

The host asked the operator, "How sensitive is that thing? And what else can you find?"

The radar operator responded: "Top of the line units are so sensitive that a skilled technician can detect a knife or fork buried four feet deep."

I was jarred out of my sleep-deprived, hypnotic state. With this I could easily find the coins! I ran into the bedroom and woke Randi: "Where can we get a Ground Penetrating Radar machine?" It was 2:00 a.m., she thought I was crazy and went back to sleep. For my part, I spent the next hour on the computer looking up places to buy a Ground Penetrating Radar machine. I didn't find any. Finally, at 3:00 a.m. I realized that the mare I was watching was not going to foal that morning and went to bed. In ensuing years, with experience, we became much better at predicting the exact day of foaling and consequently spent a lot fewer sleepless nights waiting up for a mare that wasn't yet ready to foal. Foaling seasons became much easier.

I learned that a Ground Penetrating Radar machine was not something that I could find at the local Radio Shack or on eBay and I certainly wouldn't be able to successfully operate one. Interestingly, while writing this book, I recently looked one up on the eBay: they actually had a used unit available for ten thousand dollars. Had this been the case fifteen years prior, I might have bought it. At that time, they were selling in the hundred thousand dollars and up range.

I decided I needed a professional operator and would have to find one and convince him to come on the quest with me. I first contacted the History Channel and got an address for the Underground Berlin organization. I wrote to them and told them my story and asked if they had any interest in finding buried coins in Poland. They wrote back to me that they strictly operated in Germany and had no ability to go into Poland. They also sarcastically stated that every Holocaust survivor's offspring has a story of a fortune buried in the backyard of the family home. I thanked them for their advice and expertise in the matter and moved on.

The next person I contacted was a Jewish genealogist named Arthur Kurzweil. He had written a book about tracing Jewish roots in Poland called *From Generation to Generation* and had spent much time there himself. I met him in Detroit while he was on a book tour and was speaking at the Detroit Jewish Community Campus' annual book fair and sale. I enthusiastically outlined my research and experiences in Poland and asked him if he had any advice or contacts that might be interested in doing an archeological dig. His response was that he wished he had a dollar for every fairytale that he had heard about a Jewish family's buried treasure back in Poland because then he wouldn't have to be doing the book tour circuit and answering stupid questions. In spite of his attitude, I bought his book anyway.

Life continued down on the farm and the following spring we were expecting our second crop of foals. During another all-night foal watch, now in 2003, I was watching another television show on, of course, the History Channel which gave me an idea on how to proceed with the coin quest. The show was a documentary movie called *Blood from a Stone.* It was the true story of Yaron Svoray, an Israeli ex-police detective who after retirement became an investigative journalist specializing in lost, plundered Nazi artifacts and treasure. In this documentary, Svoray is contacted by an American army veteran named Sam Nyer, who tells him the story about diamonds that he found in the possession of a dead SS soldier while fighting in a French town. Sam took the diamonds and carried them with him throughout his advance through the French countryside. These were huge uncut diamonds and the GI hid them in his underwear. They became very uncomfortable and he realized that he could not carry on with them. He buried them in a foxhole somewhere along the German border with the plan of returning after the war to retrieve them. Sam Nyer was later severely wounded in battle and was shipped stateside to recover from his injuries. The diamonds were never retrieved. After hearing Nyer's story, Svoray began a protracted and expensive search to locate the foxhole containing the diamonds. After eleven years, he was ultimately successful. His quest reminded me much of my own. I thought to myself, this would be the perfect guy to work with me on my coin quest. He acted on the word and fifty-year-old memory of a soldier; certainly he would listen to me. He also had established a list of contacts in Europe that could aid in a coin recovery operation.

I attempted to contact Yaron Svoray in Israel but was unsuccessful. I decided to enlist the help of my cousin, Ari, who also lived in Israel. Earlier, I had mentioned that some of my mother's family had left Krakow to move to Palestine, so although I have no immediate family, I do have some second cousins in Israel.

In 1933 my mother's eighteen-year-old first cousin, David, an ardent Zionist, left Poland and moved to Tel Aviv. One year later in 1934, his parents Shlomo and Stefania along with their other two children, Rena and Hirsh, decided to follow him. David's father Shlomo and my mother's father, Edward, were brothers. Shlomo had been a successful furrier in Krakow but resolved to sell his business to follow his son. In addition to wanting to reunite his family, he saw that there were troubling signs ahead for Jews in Europe. In 1936, my mother's parents, Edward and Felicja, also wanted to leave Krakow with their children due to the growing threat Adolf Hitler represented and the rise of European anti-Semitism. Unfortunately, at the time when they were considering emigrating, the Arab Revolt in Palestine was underway. It lasted three years and was in protest of Jewish immigration to Palestine. Arabs were raiding Jewish neighborhoods: looting and killing. Hundreds of Jews were ultimately killed. In 1936 Shlomo wrote the following to Edward:

There is malaria here. It is a hot and oppressive climate. It is tough to make a living and the Arabs are a major threat to our safety, we don't have any peace or quiet. The Arabs are going to be a permanent problem here; Hitler is temporary. Stay in Poland—you will be ultimately better off.

Regrettably, Edward, against his better judgement, followed Shlomo's advice and remained in Krakow.

Back in Palestine, the Arab Revolt was quelled by August 1939, which by then was too late for Edward and his family. The Germans would go on to conquer and occupy Poland in one month's time.

David went on to join the Jewish Brigade of the British Army and after the end of World War II, became a well-known architect. His sister Rena began working for the Jewish Council of Palestine and joined the Israeli government after the formation of the State of Israel in 1948. She eventually rose to hold a very influential position in the government: she was division head of the State Comptroller's Office. Shlomo and his wife both died in the early 1960s of natural causes. David's younger brother Hirsh died in 1964 after suffering a heart attack. He was forty years old.

Rena had three sons: Menachem, Yaakov, and Ari. Menachem and Yaakov were twins; their father and Rena's first husband, Leon, was killed in 1948 in Israel's War of Independence. Four years later Rena married David, a Polish Holocaust survivor and Leon's younger brother. Ari was their only child. I became close with Ari. Ari was the type of guy who could get anything done. After I asked him to help me locate Yaron Svoray, within forty-eight hours, I received a phone call from Mr. Svoray himself asking, "You are looking for me? What do you want?"

Yaron Svoray

Yaron came across as a typical Israeli on the phone. He was impatient and strictly business. There were no niceties exchanged. He just wanted to get right to the point. I told him that I believed that there was a strong possibility that I knew the location of a cache of coins in Lodz, Poland. I went on to tell him the story of how and why they were buried by my father and grandfather just prior to their deportation by the Nazis in 1939. He then asked me several obvious questions which I could not answer:

1. What are the coins worth?
2. What did your grandfather do before the war?
3. Were they rich before the war?
4. What are you willing to spend to spend to recover the coins?

These obvious questions hit me like a ton of bricks! They got me thinking and re-evaluating: what was I really doing this for? Was I hoping to get rich by finding these coins? Was it just a personal quest to prove that they were there? Was I trying to connect with a lost family long since dead? Or, was it something else? I am the son of Holocaust survivors—I admittedly have some demons. I have read that a lot of children of Holocaust Survivors suffer from obsessive, compulsive disorder. Am I one of them? I always scored in the top one percentile in standardized intelligence testing during my school years. I thought I was just smarter than everyone else and had a higher desire to seek knowledge. Maybe that's why I am doing this. I have been forging ahead with this quest for years and I have never asked myself nor tried to answer these pertinent questions. I am a successful veterinarian and have always carefully planned every step of my career with sound financial reasoning and analysis and here, with these coins, I have been running around Europe on a whim for almost twenty years with no real assessment of the value or cost of what I was chasing. Was it a hobby? Was it an obsession? Or, was it a sound business decision? What was I willing to spend?

I told Yaron that I needed some time to think about all these questions. In the meantime, he asked me to put together a detailed summary of my evidence for concluding that the coins were in Lodz. He said he would then do some research of his own and then let me know whether he had any interest in being involved in attempting to recover the coins.

My first step was to put together a convincing case that the coins were in Lodz. This is what I sent him:

Dear Yaron, I believe the coins are in Lodz and these are the facts of the case that has led me to that conclusion. These facts are indisputable:

1. When I was a boy, my father told me that his family buried a coin collection in the backyard before the Nazis kicked them out of their home.

2. My mother told me that after the war my father went back to his hometown to dig up coins that they had buried when the Nazis invaded Poland.

3. My father was born in Lodz, according to several witnesses, including a man named Izzy Oliwek who claims he was his neighbor. The man's description of the home matched what we saw when we visited Lodz. Unfortunately, Izzy Oliwek has since died.

4. In December 1939, my father along with his family was deported from Lodz to Krosno, Poland. The deportation order allowed the family to take no more than three hundred zlotys and a ten-kilogram bag of possessions per person, under penalty of death.

5. The German invaders promised the deported families that they could return to their homes in Lodz after the war. I am assuming my father's family believed their word to be true.

   Therefore, I have concluded that my father's family buried these coins in Lodz prior to being deported to Krosno. It is unlikely that the coins could have been taken with them because of their weight and value.

6. In the unlikely event that they did take the coins with them to Krosno, I doubt that they would have had any of them left over. They lived in the Krosno Ghetto for three years with no income and faced starvation every day before being executed. Surely, they would have long since exhausted any supply of money.

7. Since my father did return to Poland to unearth coins, they surely were buried at the onset of the war and not later. The family was

not able to access the Lodz coins to spend them during their years in Krosno.

I think the coins are still buried in Lodz. I do not have any fantasies about getting rich. I am in this for the sake of history.

Mark

I really wanted these coins, but I had to decide what I was willing to spend to find them. I had always done my own searching while on vacation or as a hobby, but now Yaron was hinting at possibly spending large sums of money to retrieve them. In order to commit to this, I had to attempt to find out my grandfather's financial status. Plus, I was still feeling a measure of doubt that the coins were still there. Maybe my mother was correct: perhaps they had been dug up a long time ago.

I needed to determine what my grandfather did for a living in Lodz. Was he successful enough to have had a valuable coin collection? One thing I did know was that my father had gone back to Lodz after surviving the camps to retrieve the coins. Did that confirm their value? He was obviously taking a great risk to return home to Lodz after the war. He was, on the other hand, only fourteen years old when the coins were buried: would he have had a realistic concept of what they were worth?

I first approached my mother to see what she knew about my grandfather. She thought that he may have owned a small mattress factory. But she wasn't really sure. She did say that I should look through the Wiedergutmachung file that she still had in her possession, perhaps it would have some of the information that I was looking for. I asked her, what is a Wiedergutmachung file? She said they were the reparation papers she and my father filed with the German government after the war. She showed me about two dozen letters that she had saved in an old shoe box, mixed in with the two hundred boxes of shoes that she had stored in her closet. My mother had stowed these letters in a shoe box during the 1950s and early 1960s and had not thought of them since. They were letters between the attorney in New York that was representing my mother and father and the German government attempting to resolve reparation claims. They were a treasure trove of information: they detailed both my parent's camp experiences and their movements through the concentration camp system. Included in these papers, I found the letter my father sent to Klara Hirsch in New York asking her to attest to witnessing the murders of his mother and two sisters.

I could not believe it! Information that took me fifteen years and thousands of miles to amass was sitting in my mother's possession all along.

I asked her: "Why did you not tell me that you had all these papers?"

She said: "I forgot. I put these away forty years ago."

In these papers, my dad stated that he was from Lodz. Finally, it was confirmed right from him: He was from Lodz!

I showed this paper to my mother and asked her: "Do you still think Dad is from Krosno?"

"Yes, we had a stupid lawyer. He didn't know what he was doing." She said.

In my mother's defense, some of the information in my father's letters was inaccurate. Many times he had been moved without being told of his destination. With all of the trauma that he had experienced, it is not surprising that his recollection of dates and places was somewhat imprecise. Consequently, the information he provided did not always agree with the official records that the German's had kept. It is now widely known how meticulously the Germans kept track of the concentration camp prisoners.

From our perspective, when reading these letters, the absolute lack of compassion and remorse shown by the officials representing the German government was surprising to Randi and me. They disputed compensation claims down to the day, of time spent in forced labor. Letters went back and forth before even the smallest of claims would be paid. Ironically, the Germans asked for detailed letters describing exact dates and locations of forced labor, requiring survivors to relive these experiences, even though they had this information all along.

Unfortunately, the Germans did not compensate for confiscated homes, businesses, or properties in foreign countries, including Poland, so none of my grandfather's financial information or holdings was included in these claims and therefore nothing about him was mentioned.

I then called Albert White and asked him if my dad ever mentioned anything about what his father did back in Lodz. He said that he did remember my dad mentioning something about a mattress factory. Since I heard this from two separate sources (Albert and my mother), I concluded that my grandfather probably was indeed a mattress factory owner. What was a small factory owner worth in Lodz in those days?

I wrote to Yaron Svoray and told him that my grandfather was most probably a small factory owner in Lodz. That was the only financial information that I could come up with; I hoped that it would be enough to help him in his decision to become involved in the coin quest.

A few days later, I got an email back from Yaron. In his responding e-mail, he said that he had made several calls to his contacts in Poland as well as a few American TV networks to gauge their level of interest. The answers, he claimed, were all very positive. He also spoke to experts at Yad Vashem, the Holocaust museum in Jerusalem, asking them what they thought the coins could be worth. Although they obviously could not provide an answer without knowing the type of coins. They did say that the coins are much more valuable because of the story attached to them.

Yaron said he had come up with a plan to recover the coins and asked if I could meet him in New York to pitch the story to some network executives. I agreed; I wanted to go to New York anyway because I had read that the New York Public Library had a huge collection of old European phone books, including two 1930s Polish editions. Although very few phones existed in prewar Lodz, I was hoping to find a listing for the "Biederman Mattress Company."

In addition to the Wiedergutmachung letters that my mother gave me, there was also in that same collection of documents a "Provisional Identification Card for Civilian Internee of Mauthausen" made out for my father. It was issued August 6, 1945. Mauthausen had been a concentration camp just outside of Linz, Austria. This document puzzled me greatly then and still does to this day. I know for a fact that my father was liberated from Schindler's relocated factory in Brunnlitz, Czech Republic on May 8, 1945. This is evident from the Schindler's List which was recorded that day: he was the third person on that list. If his coins were buried in Lodz, I would imagine

My father's identification papers issued from Mauthausen Concentration Camp.

that his immediate goal would be to retrieve them. Why would he make a side trip to Linz, Austria which was in the opposite direction from Brunnlitz?

I always assumed that he went directly to Lodz to unearth the coins; now I have proof of him going in the opposite direction. If indeed he did go to Lodz first, then why go to Austria at all. I know for a fact that he met my mother in Krakow, Poland in October of 1945. It wouldn't be sensible for him to travel from the Czech Republic to Poland, then to Austria and then back to Poland.

Over a period of five months, my father was in Brunnlitz, Czech Republic in May; Linz, Austria in August and Krakow, Poland in October— when did he go to Lodz? Also, what was the reason for the detour to Linz? I have no answers to this question, only wild speculation.

One possible explanation was that he was part of a group that left Brunnlitz and accompanied Oscar and Emilie Schindler on their escape from the advancing Red Army toward the American lines. Schindler felt that as a war profiteer and member of the Nazi party, he could have been summarily executed by the Soviets. As depicted at the end of the *Schindler's List* movie, he had all the prisoners sign a document attesting to his heroic efforts to save his Jewish workers. In order to make the document more believable, he had a group of Schindler Jews who were willing to act as witnesses, accompany him as he fled westward. The Schindler group's ultimate goal was to make it to neutral Switzerland where one of the Schindler Jews had relatives residing. He correctly figured that if intercepted by the Americans, they would be much more understanding than the Soviets. I have read conflicting accounts of how many Jews accompanied Schindler and the escape route they took. In Thomas Kenneally's book, *Schindler's List*, he claims they were detained for a time at Mauthausen by American military police. Historians have disputed Kenneally's account as fiction. In none of the accounts that I have read has my father been named as one of the Schindler Jews who accompanied Oscar on his escape route. As much as I would like to believe it, this explanation is pure speculation.

Unfortunately, I have not found any person, including my mother, who knows what my dad did during those five months immediately after liberation. This will probably go down as one of those permanently unanswered questions that I spoke about in my introduction. My biggest regret is that I never sat down with my father to discuss the Holocaust and his own personal history during that period. One thing was for certain: I wanted to find the coins more than ever. And I was becoming less confident of anything.

New York: July 2003

We decided to drive to New York to meet Svoray and departed Windsor at the end of July. The 9/11 attacks on the World Trade Center Towers lingered in Randi's memory and she still was not prepared to board an airplane, especially one headed to New York. I had a lot of time to think things over during the ten-hour drive. My main concern was how much information I should share with Yaron and whomever else we were going to meet with. Up until now, I only told him the city (Lodz), where I believed that the coins were buried. I was careful not to divulge the 7 Zeglarska Street address and I was pretty confident that there wasn't any way that he could obtain this information without me. Like my dad, I had a hard time trusting anyone, especially strangers. In fact, I was thinking of telling Svoray to cancel the whole thing and finding another way myself. In the end, I decided I would meet with him but avoid giving him any information that would allow him to proceed without me.

Our first stop when we arrived in New York City was the New York Public Library Annex on 43rd Street. According to Arthur Kurzweil's book, *From Generation to Generation*, it was the location where the 1930s European phone books were kept. I was hoping to find a Lodz listing including phone number and street address for my grandfather's factory to validate that it even existed. If indeed it did exist, armed with a street address, I could then determine what type of building he had: a small store-front or a substantial manufacturing facility. There were two sets of Polish phone books in the collection, just as Kurzweil described: one was Warsaw district and the other one was the rest of Poland. Unfortunately, I did not find anything under the Biederman name in either edition.

While at the library, I decided to do some further research on prewar Lodz. I found information about an Alfred Biedermann who was a textile factory owner and chemist and was the wealthiest man in Lodz prior to World War I. I got really excited! Was he a relative? My temporary euphoria was dashed as I read on and found a picture of his gravestone in the

Lodz Christian Cemetery with a large cross on it. He was definitely not related to me. I wondered, however, if I could pull off the ruse that I was Alfred's long-lost heir, when and if I returned to Lodz. His former home is called "Alfred Biedermann's Palace" and was donated to the University of Lodz and currently houses the Art History Department and the Institute of Contemporary Culture. This confusion between the Jewish Biederman and the Christian Biedermann would come into play later.

The following day, we were scheduled to meet Yaron Svoray at the Fox News headquarters on the Avenue of the Americas. The security was tight at Fox: we had to show identification and then we were issued passes to enter. It was a good start—at least our names were on the guest list to gain admission to the building. From there, we were escorted to the news room where we were scheduled to meet Yaron for the first time. He told me to look for the bald-headed guy who looked more like a Turkish Olympic wrestler than a journalist. It was an accurate description. We were given a quick tour of the Fox Studios and then taken to meet Pierre Kawka who was the senior editor of Fox News. Yaron told me that he and Pierre were longtime friends and Fox was interested in doing a story on the coin quest. Yaron had given Pierre a brief summary of my story and now wanted me to present it in greater detail.

I sat down with Randi, Yaron and Pierre and his assistant and proceeded to give what I thought was a brilliant and convincing synopsis of my research. I told him about my father telling me that there had been coins buried in the backyard and my mother saying how he went to retrieve them after the war. I also told him how I found Izzy Oliwek and learned that my dad was from Lodz. I went on to tell him about the Eichmann order and the deportation of my father's family and why I concluded that the coins were still in Lodz. While I was telling the story, it appeared that Kawka and his assistant were quite captivated by what they were hearing. I thought I was presenting the story well and that it was really coming alive to them. I was impressed with myself.

After I had finished with my dissertation I expected Kawka to say something like: "Wow, Mark, amazing! Let's go to Lodz and start digging." Instead, I got quite the opposite response. His first question to me was, "What do you do for a living?" I told him that I was an equine veterinary surgeon. His response was: "Can you not make a living at that?" I responded that I was doing quite well, thank you. He then said, "Well, I suggest you go back and make a living as a veterinarian and stop wasting your time and mine with this story." Kawka further added that his grandmother was also a Holocaust Survivor and he had heard *bubbameisah* (in Yiddish, literally grandmother's gibberish; figuratively, bullshit) like this many times before. He continued, "Everybody who is the descendant of a Holocaust survivor has a story of a fortune left in their backyard in the old country." He then called security and told them that his visitors were ready to leave. He had us escorted out of the building.

On the way out, Yaron yelled, "Don't worry about this; I'll get back to you."

Randi was devastated. I, myself, took it in stride. I figured nothing ventured, nothing gained; you can't expect to achieve anything if you never take any risks.

On the walk back to our hotel, we passed a man rolling on the sidewalk with a briefcase handcuffed to his wrist. It turns out he was a bank manager and he was cuffed to the case by a prospective bank robber. The robber said that the case contained explosives which he would detonate if not given access to the bank vault. In the end, the police freed the bank manager and the robber was apprehended a block away. The briefcase ended up containing cut up broomsticks painted red and a tangle of wires designed to look like a bomb. After looking at the bank manager writhing and dripping with sweat, I told Randi that our day was not so bad. It could have been worse.

Over the next day, we did some tourist stuff: Statue of Liberty, Ellis Island, Carnegie Deli, and the Jewish Historical Museum in Battery Park. Our trip to New York was not a complete loss.

As we were driving home, I received a call from Yaron, "I've got another idea. I will email you in a few days." I was tempted to tell him to shove his email, but regrettably, I did not.

Maidstone, Ontario: 2003

I was back at home, making a living as an equine veterinarian. After two weeks, I received the promised email from Yaron telling me not to be discouraged by the New York visit and that he is working on a plan. He said he would get back to me shortly.

Three months went by and I heard nothing from Yaron. Just as I was about to give up on him, I received a detailed three-page email of his plan. To summarize: It involved posing as film makers doing a movie shoot in Lodz focusing on World War II. The plan was to send a "fixer" to scout locations. The fixer would go to numerous locations around the city and then finally zero in on my father's street. He would then go to several residents and ask if they'd mind if we used their properties for a day of filming. They would be offered compensation for the use of their properties. Following up, a few weeks later, a film crew would arrive and locate the perfect spot for the necessary scenes. Of course, the best spot on that street would be my father's backyard.

In the next phase, the actual "filming" would take place. The director would tell the homeowner that we needed to erect a canvas barrier around the house to keep gawkers and background noise to a minimum. A little digging would also be necessary to erect the sets. This would arouse little suspicion since there is always some construction on movie sets. During this phase, the actual search for the coins would take place and since we already set up a movie set, everything would be there for an actual documentary to be filmed about the history of the coins and their discovery. At that time, I would be present for the digging and filming. Yaron wanted to put this plan in motion in one month's time. The entire operation was scheduled to take two to three months. All the necessary permits would be obtained, and everything would be legitimate. The coins, when found would be packed in with the movie equipment and taken out of the country. Yaron included a cost summary which was basically what an onsite shoot for an independent documentary movie production would cost. The cost estimate was just over hundred thousand dollars.

Although I thought that the plan was quite creative—brilliant, really—I was not ready to commit to spending such a large sum of money. Second thoughts about the likelihood of the coins still being buried in the yard on Zeglarska Street started to enter my mind. If my father and his friend went back to Lodz after the war to dig up the coins, they must have had digging equipment (shovels, spades?) with them. When the Pole who lived in the house spotted them and shot at them, at what stage of the digging were they? If the hole was partially dug, he would have known that they had come to dig up valuables, and they had unwittingly revealed the location. Even if they had not begun digging, the Polish resident would have a dead body on his property, with possibly a shovel in his possession. Did my dad have the time and foresight to escape and retrieve the digging tools? Did the Pole see the digging tools? Even without a Ground Penetrating Radar machine, once he had concluded that there was something of value there, he has had sixty years to dig the yard up, inch by inch. I was leaning towards believing that the coins were no longer there, especially since my mother said that my father never went back after the shooting incident. He probably concluded the same thing: that he had given the secret away.

About a week after I received Yaron's email, he called me and said he was coming to the Detroit area to give a speech about the *Blood from a Stone* documentary. He suggested that we meet and talk further about the coin recovery plan. By now, my enthusiasm was lukewarm but I agreed to meet with him anyway.

In December 2003, I met Yaron in Detroit and told him that I had concerns about whether or not the coins were still there. At that point in time, I was not ready to commit hundred thousand or more dollars to this project. He told me that even without finding the coins that the documentary still would have value. I disagreed: I remembered Geraldo Rivera and his infamous Al Capone empty vault documentary. He was a laughing stock and the show was a bust. In no way was I going to spend a significant amount of money to become involved in an embarrassing situation like that.

Yaron understood my trepidation, but still wanted to explore some other possibilities. He told me he was going to Poland for another purpose and would do the fixer role himself, at no upfront cost to me. He said that we could worry about sorting out expenses later. At this point, I was ready to disclose the address of my father's childhood home. I had pretty much shelved the idea, for now, that I was going back to Poland and figured I had nothing to lose. This was the first time that Yaron heard the words: Zeglarska 7. I also suggested that it would be much cheaper to simply approach the homeowner and offer him a fee to allow us to dig in his yard. We did need to find someone who had a Ground Penetrating Radar machine. I figured that there must have been treasure hunters and archeologists in Poland just like the Underground Berlin guys in Germany. He dismissed that idea. He had concerns that it would be unsafe. Once valuable coins were found, the homeowner might not be satisfied with his fee, and a dangerous situation could ensue. Plus, once we asked to dig, he would say no and dig it himself, realizing that something of significance was there.

Yaron said he would call me after he returned from Poland and we could discuss further planning. It never happened. This would be the last time that I would ever see Yaron Svoray or discuss finding the coins again. He no longer needed me, I had revealed to him where the coins were located.

Wednesday April 21, 2004: Maidstone, Ontario

I was on farm calls seeing equine patients when I received a phone call on my cell phone. It was Yaron. I could barely make out who it was or hear him. There was a lot of commotion in the background: there was a lot of yelling and screaming. He said to me: "Hi Mark, I am on Zeglarska Street and I found your coins."

I was completely stunned. I did not know what to say. When I finally regained my composure, I asked him: "What happened to getting back to me?"

He replied, "Well, I told you I was going to be in Poland, so I figured I would just ask the mayor for permission to dig, just to see what he'd say. Surprisingly, he agreed. So, we decided to dig." He then said he had to go and handed his phone off to a Polish newspaper reporter named Joanna Podolska who wanted to speak with me. I have never seen or spoken to Yaron since.

Joanna asked me if I would be coming to Poland to claim the coins. My answer was, "Of course!" She gave me her phone number and said to call her when I make the travel arrangements and she would meet me in Lodz and explain everything that happened and recommend how to proceed from there. She said that she was interested in doing a feature story on me, the coin story, and my father's family. She also asked if I would mind if a Polish television crew followed along. I told her I would have no problems with a television crew.

After I hung up, I quickly finished with my patient and called Randi at work. I told her that Yaron called and said that he found the coins. Randi was initially elated that the coins had been found but that quickly disintegrated into disgust with Yaron that he went and dug them up without including me or even telling me that there was a plan in place. And then she said, "You are going to Poland."

The rest of the day was surreal. I was still out on farm calls and was telling all of my clients about the coin discovery. Someone notified the news services and when I got back to the clinic, there were three television reporters from local networks and a *Windsor Star* newspaper reporter waiting for me. Due to the time difference in Poland, the news had already broken across Europe. There was a story on Poland 1 TV as well as the BBC. The video of the coin search and pictures were available on the City of Lodz website. On the six o'clock local news, the story ran as the lead story. At 11:00 p.m., my story was also the lead on CBC national news.

The following morning Randi booked my flight to Poland. I was to leave on the evening of Monday, April 26 and land in Warsaw on Tuesday morning. From Warsaw, I planned to take a train to Lodz the following day. After booking my trip, I notified Joanna Podolska of my travel arrangements. She agreed to meet me at the Lodz train station on Wednesday morning, with her news team and a television crew. After I hung up with Joanna, I received a call from a woman named Eva who said that she was the assistant to the Israeli Ambassador to Poland in Warsaw. She asked me if I was scheduled to come to Poland to attempt to retrieve the coins and if so, she wanted to meet with me. She gave me her cell phone number and asked me to call her as soon as I arrived in Poland. After I hung up, I wondered, what does the Israeli Embassy want with me?

On the Sunday before I left, I went to visit my mother to tell her everything that had happened in the previous few days and inform her that I was going back to Poland. I was expecting an excited response at my accomplishment, but instead, she said, "What are you going to Lodz for? Those aren't your coins. Your dad was from Krosno. Those are somebody else's coins."

After visiting my mother, I stopped at the cemetery where my father was buried. I was still in such disbelief that after twenty years of trying, the coins had been located. I just sat near my father's grave thinking about everything he'd been through, all the suffering and the murdered family members and now all I have are a few coins. I was melancholy.

Poland: April 2004

The following evening I flew out of Detroit. After a stopover in Schiphol Airport in Amsterdam, I landed in Warsaw the next morning. It was a really bad time to be in Warsaw: the European Economic Summit was being held there and the city was on edge expecting violent protests. Security was tight, and many streets were closed off. I arrived exhausted and had a four-hour taxi ride into town because of all the detours. I checked into the Warsaw Marriott, got something to eat and called it a night: I had a big day tomorrow.

On Wednesday morning, April 28, I walked to the train station and purchased a ticket to Lodz. The train ride was very eerie. As we passed rural hamlets, there were railway sidings which had abandoned wooden rail cars which resembled the German cattle cars used to transport Jews to the death camps, rusting in place. I felt like I had gone back in time. I was wondering if I was seeing things. I was jet lagged and sleep deprived. I really hadn't slept since the discovery of the coins.

When the average person visits Europe, they see beautiful scenery, baroque buildings, romantic villages, think of classical music and soak in the ambiance. For me, I see Jewish suffering and death. I often wondered if other descendants of survivors or any Jews for that matter feel the same way. Or do they just enjoy Europe? I still feel robbed of the ability to enjoy myself while visiting this continent. When visiting Paris, the average tourist sees the Eiffel Tower and appreciates an amazingly beautiful structure and feat of engineering; I see Adolf Hitler standing on the viewing platform and I envision him thinking, "How am I going to kill all the Jews in this country?" As I was trying to distract myself from the Holocaust imagery in my mind, I struck up a conversation with the very attractive woman sitting next to me.

She told me that she was a famous European actress originally from Lodz, now living in Paris. She never did tell me her name. She said that she was returning to Lodz as the guest of honor for the Lodz International Film Festival. After the war, Lodz had become an Eastern European film mecca and was the home of the International Film School of Lodz which was founded in 1948. Roman Polanski, disgraced, formerly internationally acclaimed film director, was among the more notable alumni. Interestingly, Polanski was living in Krakow when the war broke out and he and his family were eventually forced into the Krakow Ghetto and lived in the same building as my mother and her family.

About a half hour prior to arriving in Lodz, the actress pulled out her cosmetic case and began fixing her hair and applying makeup. She told me not to disturb her during her preparation. As we pulled into the Fabryczna station, we could see Joanna and the other reporters and television crew waiting on the platform for me. The actress, assuming that they were paparazzi and were there to see her, asked me to let her get off the train first and told me to stay at least ten meters behind her so that no one would think I was with her. She didn't want any rumors starting that I was her boyfriend and she told me, "You know how the press can be." I let her get off first and hung back the required ten meters. As she was walking along the platform, I stepped off the train and all the reporters rushed towards me, right past her. She turned to see what they were running to: it was me! She dropped her cosmetic bag and with a stunned look on her face, tried to make sense of just what happened. I am not a good Polish lip reader, but I think she said, "Who the hell are you?"

I met all of the reporters and crew on the railway platform. Mercifully, they all spoke perfect English. They filmed my arrival in Lodz as I stepped down from the train. They were very happy with the dramatic scene of a surviving Biederman descendant returning to Lodz. After exiting the train station, we got into a van and drove to Zeglarska Street. At the site, Joanna showed me where the coins had been found. My first thought was: Damn! They were exactly where I thought they would have been. They were next to a large tree, adjacent to the alley. The tree would have obstructed the neighbors' view of the spot. I thought to myself, I could have come out here myself one night and dug these up clandestinely and then I would have the coins and not have to deal with any of this. At that time, I did not mind being a celebrity veterinarian but the Holocaust was personal and internal for me. Over time, I have become more open about my family and their past but at that time, it was a struggle. As I gave it more thought, I realized I did not want to end up shot like my father's friend and I'm glad I did not attempt anything crazy.

It was a grey, dreary, cold day in Lodz. As I stared at the hole in the ground that the coins had been resting in for sixty-five years, I started having images of my father as a boy of fourteen on that December 4, 1939 night digging alongside his father. Little did his father Leopold know, I thought, that he would never see Lodz again and what horrors awaited him and the rest of the family. I also pictured my father as a twenty-year-old returning in 1945 with his friend and watching his friend being shot. I wondered, was this the spot where the friend lay dying? Did he escape and die later in a hospital? What happened to the friend's body? Is it buried somewhere in the yard? I broke down and sobbed. I was ready to tell Joanna, take me back to the train station. I just wanted to go home.

After about fifteen minutes, I was able to regain my composure and continue. We spent about an hour at Zeglarska Street, filming the yard and talking about the story of how I discovered the location of the coins and the tragic post war shooting of my father's friend. At noon the crew wanted to break for lunch. We went to the local Pizza Hut. I never realized that pizza was so popular in Poland and corn seems to be the number one topping. I hadn't ever had corn on a pizza in North America before, but I must say, it is actually a pretty good garnish! During the lunch, Joanna began to tell me the story of how Yaron went about unearthing the coins.

In 2004, the city of Lodz was hosting a yearlong schedule of events to commemorate the sixtieth anniversary of the liquidation of the Lodz Ghetto and the murder of the city's 250,000 Jews. The Lodz Ghetto was established in December 1939 shortly after the initial deportations of Jews to the General Government. As previously mentioned, my father's family had been part of these initial deportations and consequently never saw the inside of the Lodz Ghetto. These deportations did not go as efficiently as the Nazis would have liked. It was therefore decided that the Jews of Lodz should be separated and isolated from the rest of the population into a ghetto to make the future round ups easier. The place selected to be the ghetto was in a part of the Baluty section of the city. It was a particularly shabby district just north of the main municipal center. All the non-Jewish residents were ordered to leave this area and all the Lodz Jews were ordered to move in beginning on December 10, 1939. The relocation was completed in May 1940, and the ghetto inhabitants were officially sealed in by fence and brick walls. The Lodz Ghetto became the first large scale metropolitan prison of its kind and became the model for future ghettos throughout Nazi occupied Europe. Over the next several months, little by little, Jews from the ghetto were deported the fifty miles northwest to the Nazi death camp in Chelmno and gassed to death using diesel exhaust. While the deportations were taking place, the Nazis restarted the numerous textile factories already located within the Ghetto to employ the Jews awaiting deportation. The Jewish workers received food rations in return for their labor. In August 1944, the final liquidation of the Ghetto was ordered and the remaining 75,000 Jews were sent to Auschwitz where most were immediately gassed upon arrival. A few Jews were selected to remain in the Ghetto to clean it up and restore it to habitable conditions for potential future use by German civilians. Due to rapid decline in Germany's fortunes of war, this would never happen. German forces were retreating rapidly, and the Reich was ever shrinking. Five months later, on January 19, 1945 the Red Army liberated the Lodz Ghetto. Of the original 250,000 Jewish residents who were interned, only 877 were left in the Ghetto to be liberated.

As part of the planned commemorative events, in April 2004, there was a scheduled walk of young Israelis around the perimeter of the former Ghetto. Yaron and Fox News senior editor, Pierre Kawka arrived ostensibly to do a documentary of the Lodz Ghetto and the Israeli delegation's visit. Yaron went to the city hall to get the necessary permits for the documentary. While there, Yaron mentioned to the mayor that he had an acquaintance back in Canada named Mark Biederman. Mark's grandfather, Yaron said, had been a factory owner in Lodz and had buried some coins in his residence's backyard in Lodz. "Alfred Biedermann?" asked the mayor, referring to the wealthy pre-World War I Christian industrialist. Yaron shrugged; he didn't know who Alfred was. He told the mayor that he didn't know my grandfather's name, but he asked if he could search the property for the coins. After some consultation with the Ministry of Culture, the mayor agreed provided that anything found would become property of the Polish government. Yaron and Pierre agreed to the terms.

Soon after Yaron's meeting with the Lodz mayor, rumors spread that an American film crew was in town to dig up Alfred Biedermann's coin collection.

On the day that the dig was scheduled, Yaron and Kawka were to meet the mayor and his team of officials at city hall and proceed to the dig site. The mayor and his team wanted to be present to oversee the dig. Yaron arrived with his film crew and a Ground Penetrating Radar operator whom he had hired. Also waiting at city hall was a large contingent of Polish media who had heard the rumors of Alfred Biedermann's coin dig.

A convoy of vehicles followed Yaron's group, expecting to be heading off to Alfred Biedermann's Palace just northeast of city hall. Instead, the convoy followed Yaron as he turned northwest on Zgierska Street toward the decidedly unfashionable Baluty district. When they arrived at the former Biederman home, the press asked Yaron, "Why would Alfred Biedermann bury his coins in this neighborhood?" At some point they came to the realization that this was another Biederman and a Jewish one at that. Because of the confusion regarding the identity of the different Biedermans, the story received much wider media attention than it ordinarily would have received.

Under renewed skepticism, after the revelation of the mistaken identity, Yaron and Kawka's crew began planning the exploration of the property. The property was divided into grids and the radar scanning begun grid by grid. In the first grid, there was a hit for a disturbance in the soil about one meter deep. As the excitement mounted, Yaron himself began to dig and at the one-meter level, he hit a box of nails, much to the disappointment of the audience. Yaron's team continued to scan the yard. Soon another disturbance was identified in the soil. This time old building materials, a few shingles and bricks were unearthed. The audience was beginning to become impatient and the mayor began mocking this crazy man and his wild adventure. A third disturbance revealed more debris. The heckling grew louder. After those three misses, Yaron had covered the entire lawn surface. Just before deciding to quit in shame, Yaron noticed a little flower garden that was behind a tree at the edge of the property. Yaron asked the homeowner if he minded them scanning over the garden. The homeowner reluctantly agreed after feeling the pressure of all these media present in his yard. Under the garden at nearly one meter, a disturbance in the soil was detected. Yaron grabbed his shovel and anxiously began to dig. As he plunged his shovel into the soil, he desperately hoped that he would find something other than discarded building materials. This was his last chance. Then, as he dug deeper, there was a clink and then a crash, the sound of steel hitting and then shattering ceramic.

Yaron stopped digging and got down on his hands and knees, he then reached into the hole and carefully removed the first coin from among the shards of broken crockery. He then stood up triumphantly and waved the 1824 Netherlands King Wilhelm ten guilder gold piece over his head to show the crowd. Everyone gasped in amazement. There really were coins here! Yaron handed the first coin to Pierre Kawka who then handed it off to the mayor for his inspection and then Yaron started gently reaching into the hole to pull out the remaining coins, one by one. As Yaron removed the second gold coin from its crypt, the mayor grabbed his chest and collapsed to the ground. As his aids rushed to assist the fallen mayor, Yaron and Kawka carried on removing the coins. Before they finished removing all the coins, an ambulance arrived to remove the mayor and spirited him off to the hospital. In all, Yaron removed sixty-three coins and also collected the remnants of what turned out to be a white ceramic teapot. The coins were then surrendered to the representative from the Ministry of Culture. From there, the coins were taken to the Museum of Archeology and Ethnography and locked in the museum's vault.

As Joanna finished telling me the story of the unearthing of the coins, she let me know that the museum will be our next stop. After lunch, the television crew returned to their studio, so it was just me, Joanna, and the cameraman from the *Lodz Gazette* on the way to the museum.

We arrived at the museum and were met at the back entrance by a security guard. We proceeded to the manager's office where the vault was located. The manager was relatively cordial, although he spoke almost no English and my ability in Polish was basic conversational. Using Joanna as an occasional interpreter, I told the tragic story of my father's ill-fated family to the manager. He listened and seemed genuinely interested. After I concluded, he went to the vault and removed a ring binder which contained the coins. He placed the binder on the desk in front of me. I picked up the binder, tucked it under my left arm and said, "Djienkuje, bardzo" (Thank you very much), and with a wave of my right hand, I turned around and headed for the door. The manager quickly grabbed my hand as the security guard blocked my path to the door. He then said in Polish, "I regret to tell you that the coins are the property of the Polish treasury."

I said, "Oh? I thought you were presenting them to me after I've just proved to you that they were property of my family."

He replied, "Polish law says otherwise." He continued to explain his understanding of Polish law and said that there are three criteria that were being used to conclude that the coins were property of the Polish Republic:

1. According to Polish law, anything found or removed from under the ground becomes the government's property. Had the coins been found on the surface, it MAY have been a different story. This law is a holdover from the Communist era. As an example, if you grow potatoes and harvest them by digging them up from the ground, they are the government's property and the government can confiscate them as they deem necessary. This is the essence of communism. So I guess, according to the museum manager, you are better off growing tomatoes in Poland.
2. There are no records whatsoever of a Biederman family ever owning the property at Zeglarska 7.
3. In order to claim lost valuables, the owner must be able to provide an accurate description of the property which matches exactly what was found.

My response to the museum manager, although I knew it was futile, was that if the Biederman family had never owned the property, how would I have known that the coins were there? Secondly, I told him that he obviously knew that there was no way I could give him an exact description of what was found since the coins were buried decades before I was born. In the end, he told me, I was more than welcome to look through them and spend as much time as I needed but by 4:00 p.m., they were going back into the vault.

Realizing that my grandparents and my aunts once had held these coins, I became very emotional. I was choked up and felt my chest tightening. I was thinking I was going to end up hospitalized with the mayor. I removed each coin from its slot, looked at each one, held it for a few seconds, felt each coin, rubbed it in my hands and then put each back. I felt like my lost family was being stolen from me once again.

The culmination of my twenty-year quest was right there, contained in this three-ring binder sitting on the desk in front of me. After replacing all the coins into their slots, I looked through the book once more, but this time from a numismatist's perspective. I was surprised that all of the coins originated from Western European countries or were of Germanic origin. There was not a Polish or Russian coin in the bunch, which was puzzling to me. Months later I would find an explanation for this. The coins ranged in date from 1702 to 1915. They were gold or silver coins and all were in uncirculated or excellent condition. I was impressed with the collection. They were much more intriguing than my 1916 Mercury Head dime.

After about an hour in the museum, we headed out and went to the *Lodz Gazette* offices. I spent about half an hour with Joanna finishing the details for her story. I showed her the pictures of my father's family which she asked me to bring to Poland. Joanna had them photocopied and told me that they would be used in a Sunday feature story which she planned on writing for a future edition. She then gave me the name and phone number of a prominent Polish restitution lawyer and asked if I would keep her apprised as to what my plans were in attempting to acquire the coins and how things were progressing. She then drove me to the train station, wished me well, and said goodbye.

While waiting for the train back to Warsaw, I called Eva from the Israeli Embassy. I used my new Polish cell phone which I bought that morning in Warsaw on the way to the train station. Prior to leaving Canada, I went to Telus Mobility to verify that my cell phone would work in Poland. They sold me an international sim card and assured me that it would work fine in Poland. Of course, it did not. I told Eva that I would be arriving in Warsaw that evening and wondered what she wanted. She said that she wanted to meet with me and discuss my plans for the coins. I told her that I could meet her at the embassy the following morning. She responded that due to heightened security because of the European Economic Conference, the embassy was closed. She offered to come and meet with me at the hotel that evening.

The train ride back to Warsaw was uneventful. I slept most of the way. I was exhausted; it was an emotionally draining day.

When I got back to the hotel, I called Eva and she arranged to meet me at the hotel restaurant and sports bar. She wanted to watch the semifinals of the EuroLeague Basketball Championships. There was an Israeli team playing. I was starving—I hadn't eaten since the Pizza Hut in Lodz.

We met at the sports bar and took a table. We ordered dinner, soft drinks and chatted a bit. Then it got serious when the conversation turned to the coins. Eva told me that this is not your father's Poland. Poland had become a strategic ally for Israel in the region. In 2003, Poland attempted to win a seat on the United Nations Security Council as a member at large but failed; however, Eva said that eventually they will succeed. She reminded me that Israel needed all the friends that they could get in the United Nations. She then went on to tell me that Polish law is very complex regarding cases like mine and it would be a long and expensive process with no guarantee of success if I made a claim for the coins. She also said, and I believe it is true to this day, that Poland is the only nation to never pay any restitution claims to Holocaust victims. Eva asked me how successful I was as a veterinarian and whether I needed the money that the coins could bring. I told her that I was doing well financially and this quest had already cost me a substantial amount of money and a huge investment in time. If I was in this for the money, I would have quit long ago after losing the first thirty dollars that I sent enclosed in letters to Krosno in 1984. Eva asked me what I was talking about: letters to Krosno? I proceeded to go through the story with her from start to finish.

After I finished the story, she was amazed at my tenacity and said she had no idea what effort had gone into this. She told me that the city of Lodz was interested in building a museum of the Holocaust and that I should consider donating the coins for the building. She said that my family's story could be the focus of the museum as the embodiment of the fate of the Jews of Lodz. Think of it, she said, generations of Lodz school children would study fate of the Biederman family. They will be synonymous with the Holocaust. What better legacy can you leave for your family?

She affirmed that the Israeli embassy would prefer not to take an official position as to the rightful ownership of the coins. I told her the Israeli embassy has no official standing anyway, as far as I was concerned. I was an American citizen and if anything, I would request assistance from the US Embassy. I told her that I did understand her concerns and realized that as a Jew, my actions would impact on the perception of the Jewish State in Poland. Eva asked me before leaving if I would at least keep her apprised as to whether or not I would seek legal remedies. I told her I would take her suggestions under advisement and keep in touch.

Eva stayed with me in the sports bar until the end of the basketball game. Israel won the game and ultimately the EuroLeague championship. She left jubilant and stuck me with the restaurant tab.

I sat in the restaurant collecting my thoughts. I just had a lot of pressure put on my shoulders. My personal coin collection now became a matter of Israeli national security. It had been an emotionally taxing few days. I needed a day off. I had two days left in Warsaw and decided to do something completely different, totally unrelated to the coins. I stopped by the concierge and inquired about a trip to East Prussia to visit Hitler's Eastern Front headquarters, the Wolf's Lair. The Wolf's Lair was the site of Von Stauffenberg's failed assassination attempt of Adolf Hitler on July 20, 1944 and in my mind, a must for World War II history buffs, like me.

The Wolf's Lair is located in northern Poland in a region that was once part of Germany. After World War II, the area known as East Prussia was divided between the Soviet Union and Poland. The Wolf's Lair was the secret Fuhrer headquarters built in a heavily wooded area and is located in the now Polish portion of the region. It is 152 miles north of Warsaw.

The concierge explained that there is no real easy way to get there and it would be best to hire a private car and driver. The Marriott had a driver whom they recommended and I was quoted a rate of four hundred dollars. I accepted and arranged to leave at 7 a.m. the following morning. I actually enjoy long car rides, and the solitude is a way for me to collect my thoughts, and for years it has been a way for me to deal with stress. I figured while on the seven-hour round trip, I would come up with some ideas of what I would do with the coins. If I decided to pursue obtaining the coins, I needed to come up with a way to rescue them.

I went up to my room at about 11:00 p.m. and just couldn't sleep. I figured I'd go for a walk. I went out the front entrance and then headed north on John Paul II Avenue and walked the two miles to the Warsaw Ghetto Uprising Monument. From there I went the short distance to Mila Street, site of the Jewish Resistance headquarters. Today a mound of rubble sits on top of the place where most of the leaders remain entombed after the Germans set fire to the underground bunkers. The address was Mila 18; we named one of our horses after it. I returned to the hotel at 3:00 a.m. As I approached the front door, the security guard stopped me, "You can't go in there."

I replied, "I am a hotel guest and showed him my key."

He was shocked: "You went out at this time of night? Here? It is unsafe to walk around this area alone at night."

My response: "Couldn't be any more dangerous than it was for a Jew in 1943." He shook his head and let me in. I finally got to bed at 3:30 a.m. I was going to be in great shape for my 6:00 a.m. wake-up call.

At 6:00 a.m., I got the wakeup call and stumbled out of bed. I went downstairs. I bought the *Lodz Gazette* because I noticed that I was pictured on the front page holding the coins. Interestingly, the caption said, "Mark Biederman with his Family's Coin Collection, unearthed at Zeglarska Street." I figured, what is the issue? It is abundantly clear that these are my coins! Common sense would tell anyone that the coins are mine, even the newspaper said so. The Polish government apparently didn't agree.

The *Lodz Gazette* does not have an English edition, so I bought the English version of the *Warsaw Voice* to keep up on world events. I wasn't fluent enough in Polish to read the *Lodz Gazette*. On the front cover of the *Warsaw Voice* there was an article about the Jedwabne Massacre of 1941.

Lodz Gazette with me and the coins.

Jedwabne

Jedwabne is a small village about one hundred miles northeast of Warsaw. It was in the Soviet zone of occupation since 1939 as agreed to by the previously mentioned Molotov-Ribbentrop Soviet-German Non-Aggression Pact. On June 22, 1941 the Germans broke the pact and attacked the Soviet Union. By July 10, 1941 German forces occupied the town of Jedwabne after it was abandoned by the fleeing Red Army. The SS Einsatzgruppen commander of the region assembled a group of local Polish men to identify the Jewish residents of the town. The Polish men were zealously willing to assist the Germans in rounding up the local Jewish population. The group originally rounded up fifty Jewish men and dragged them to the town square where they were tortured and beaten. The town rabbi's eyes were gouged out and his tongue was cut off. The fifty Jewish men were then led to a barn and killed, some were shot, some beaten to death. The incited Polish mob then rousted another four hundred Jews, including women and children and herded them to the same barn. After locking them inside, the barn was doused with kerosene and set on fire, and the people were burned alive.

After the war, the Poles blamed the Nazis for the massacre and denied that any Polish citizens had participated. A Soviet war crimes tribunal that commenced in 1945 concluded, however, that Polish citizens and not Nazis had indeed committed the murders. For many years the responsibility for the crime was a source of friction between the Western world and the Polish government. Finally in 2001, the Polish President, Aleksander Kwasnieswski, gave an apology and accepted accountability for the crime. After a two-year Polish investigation which commenced after Kwasnieswski's speech, it was concluded that Poles were indeed the perpetrators of the Jedwabne Massacre. The final report was released in 2004 which is what I was reading in the Warsaw newspaper. Many Poles still dispute this account and do not accept responsibility. They say the Germans either committed the massacre or coerced the Poles into doing it.

As I was concluding reading the article, my driver Mishkel arrived. Is every driver in Poland named Mishkel? When he saw what I was reading, he asked if I knew anything about Jedwabne. I answered that of course I did. He retorted, "There was a little disagreement there, wasn't there?" I wasn't sure what he meant. Did he mean the sixty-three-year debate as to the responsibility for the crime or did he consider the massacre of more than four hundred Jews by their Polish neighbors to constitute "a little disagreement"? I thought to myself, shit, I'm going to have fun with this asshole for the next seven hours. How about I stiff you for the four hundred dollars, and then we'll see a little disagreement between a Pole and a Jew.

Mishkel said that Jedwabne was only a thirty-mile detour from the route to the Wolf's Lair. He asked if I would be interested in going there for an extra fifty dollars. Who wouldn't want to go for fifty dollars; I agreed.

It was a beautiful, sunny spring day. We got in the car and headed out of Warsaw, north towards Jedwabne. We arrived in about ninety minutes. I asked Mishkel to stop at the town square. I wanted to see where the Jews had been beaten. Before I got out of the car, I asked Mishkel, "How is the local attitude towards Jews now?"

He said, "Fine, this is the new Poland. But, do us both a favor and tuck your Star of David pendant into your shirt."

Jedwabne today has a population of about two thousand. It features an unusual town square. As opposed to the bustling area of commerce normally seen in Eastern European town squares, this one is more like a municipal park. It consists of a grassy area rimmed by cobblestone and filled with a mixture of deciduous and coniferous trees. In the center, there is a small cobblestone area with a few park benches. Across the street from the square on the east, south, and west sides are dilapidated shops and multifamily dwellings. On the north side is the most prominent feature of Jedwabne: the twin spired Catholic Church which dates from 1737. It was in the shadows of this church that the original beatings took place in the town square in July 1941.

Mishkel parked the car on the west side of the square and we got out and walked to the middle of the square. Sitting on a park bench was an old man tossing bread crumbs to the pigeons. My first thought was, I wonder if this guy took part in the beatings and massacre. I wanted to ask him where he was in 1941 and if he witnessed the pogrom, but Mishkel suggested otherwise. I think he was afraid that I may incite another mob scene. I was amazed that something so horrible could happen here in this place and yet everyone seemed so oblivious to it and carried on with their normal daily activities like throwing bread crumbs to a pigeon. I thought to myself, it is unfortunate that the perpetrators of this heinous crime were never identified or prosecuted by the Polish authorities. Thus, as we say about the victims in Hebrew, "Hashem yinkom damam": May God avenge their blood.

We got back in the car and headed to the site where the Jews were immolated. Within a few blocks of the town center, it became very rural with old farm houses and barns. It was only four blocks from the central square to the former location of the infamous barn.

Monument defaced at Jedwabne.

As we pulled up to the site, there was a ring of concrete road blocks surrounding a stone monument where the barn once stood. The wording on the monument had been recently changed to reflect the Polish participation in the massacre. The monument was spray painted with graffiti which included a swastika. I didn't even get out of the car. I had seen enough. The coins seemed so insignificant to me at this moment.

I told Mishkel, I wanted to get out of this place as soon as possible. I couldn't wait to see Jedwabne in the rear-view mirror. Within five minutes we were back on the highway heading for the Wolf's Lair. Mishkel was silent. He seemed to pick up on my ire and toned down his sarcasm.

Driving in the rural sections of Poland was quite a unique experience. Most of the highways were two lane loosely paved roads, just wide enough for vehicles to safely pass each other. More often than not, the driver had to share the road with horse drawn wagons full of farm produce going to market. It was quite a hair-raising experience as the drivers were passing these slow-moving wagons just narrowly avoiding oncoming traffic. After four hours of this, we arrived at the Wolf's Lair.

Wolf's Lair

Unfortunately, nothing remains intact of the original structures. Von Stauffenberg's bomb destroyed one of the buildings in his failed assassination attempt, and the rest were blown up in January 1945 by the retreating German forces when the Wolf's Lair was abandoned. Their goal was to keep it from falling into the hands of the Red Army. They did not want to leave Russians a functional command post. Most interesting for me was that Hitler spent the majority of his time there during the period from summer 1942 until January 1945 and yet the Allies never knew that this place existed. The Wolf's Lair complex was discovered by the Soviets in January 1945 during their sweep through Poland towards Germany. When visiting the complex, the only things I saw were blown up concrete bunkers. Hitler's personal bunker is the one which is most intact since it was the most heavily fortified with four-foot thick concrete walls. Unless you are an extreme World War II history buff, I wouldn't recommend a visit; there isn't much to see there, especially if you are planning on making a day trip from Warsaw.

After spending about two hours walking among the ruins of the Wolf's Lair, we decided to stop for lunch before the long drive back to Warsaw. Mishkel suggested that we make the short drive to Ketrzyn and eat there. Ketrzyn, he said, has a lot of ethnic Germans living there and, therefore, had some good German restaurants. I told him I was okay with whatever restaurant he chose.

We made the short drive to Ketrzyn and stopped at a restaurant just off the highway. After we sat down, the waitress came up to me and said that she thought she had seen me on the evening news the previous night and asked if I was the guy with the coins. I said that I was. She then asked if I would mind having a picture taken with her. I told her that I would be fine with being in a picture. She excused herself and then ran to her car to get her camera. This was 2004, before every cell phone had a camera and prior to the existence of social media. She had the picture taken and then took our order and disappeared into the kitchen. A few moments later the entire restaurant staff came out and asked if they could shake my hand. They all offered congratulations to me on finding the coins. I was pleasantly surprised by the reception I received. Up until now, disdain was the usual reaction from the average Pole. Mishkel thought that the restaurant crew had mistaken me for an Irish soccer star who was now playing in the Polish league. He told me that I looked just like him and with my athletic build, I could easily pass for a professional athlete. He was not used to a foreigner, especially a Jewish foreigner receiving such a warm response.

I realized that these folks were different from the poor blue collar Lodzers or the rural Polish farmers of Jedwabne. It gave me some hope for the future of Poland. Before the war, Ketrzyn had been called Rastenburg and was a German city. Many of the residents were ethnic German or at least of mixed lineage and were quite distinct from the average Pole. Nonetheless, my disgust with Poland was temporarily suspended.

During the drive back to Warsaw I received a call on my cell phone from Joanna Podolska from Lodz. She said that she had been contacted by an editor of a Polish World War II history magazine who wanted to do a story about my father's family and my quest to find the buried coins. She said that they would meet with me in Warsaw if I would be willing to sit down for an interview. Although I was totally exhausted and emotionally drained by this time, I told her that I would agree to sit for one more interview. She said she would call me back after talking to the editor to finalize arrangements. Joanna called back promptly to let me know that the interview was scheduled for 11 a.m. the next morning in the Marriott lobby.

The rest of the car ride was rather uneventful except for the near misses of head on collisions as Mishkel passed the horse carts. He became more reckless as time went on. Quite a few times I thought that I was going to die here on a lonely stretch of Polish highway. How ironic, I thought, another Biederman snuffed out prematurely in the Polish wilderness.

In the end, we arrived safely in Warsaw and pulled into the parking lot of the Marriott hotel. I was relieved to be back. I opened my wallet and pulled out five crisp hundred-dollar bills and handed them to Mishkel. There would be no "little disagreement." It was 7:00 p.m.; I had survived twelve hours with him. We shook hands and as I got out of the car he mentioned that I can take my Star of David out of my shirt now. As I thanked him for his advice, he sped off into the night.

When I got back to my room, I called Randi to fill her in on the trip. She was disappointed that, for the time being, I was not coming home with the coins. She told me that the *Windsor Star*, CBC network, and the local television and radio news reporters had all called to inquire what happened in Poland and when I was coming home with the coins. They all wanted to see them and do a story with me when I got home. Oh shit, I thought, as if leaving the coins in Lodz wasn't bad enough, now I've got to explain my failure to secure them to the entire Canadian media. I wasn't used to failure, especially not on the national stage. I was not looking forward to dealing with them.

Before going to bed I pulled out the pictures I had of my father and his sisters in preparation for my interview the following morning.

At 3:00 a.m. I was awoken, or so I thought, by my cell phone ringing. I picked up the phone and it was my father's sister. She told me she had survived the war on forged papers and decided to continue living under the same identity until today. She said she saw my articles in the newspaper and decided to contact me. She had been living a false life for sixty-five years. I jumped out of bed. My heart was racing. Was I dreaming this? I quickly scrambled to locate my cell phone. When I found it, it was turned off. I began to think, what proof did I have that the three sisters were dead? I only had the secondhand testimony of an eyewitness already dead (Klara Hirsch). Why were there only two girls' names on the Lodz deportation list? I thought it was a transcription error when the records were computerized, but maybe not. I tried to think logically. My father remained in Europe until 1949, surely he would've known his sister was not deported and would've found her after the war. How old would the sister have been anyway? I realized I didn't have an answer to this question. I had to go back and find these records. I only knew two girls' names and wasn't even sure if they were correct. The manager at the Lodz Museum said there were no records of the Biederman family ever living at 7 Zeglarska Street. Was he lying?

The longer I thought about it, I figured it was impossible that one of the girls was still alive, but I needed to find their birthdates and ages anyway. I set that as one of my goals in 1984 and I have not yet accomplished it. I decided that's going to be the final focus of my quest. I then went back to sleep, but left my cell phone on just in case.

I woke up the next morning at 10 a.m. I was still somewhat disturbed, almost haunted by my dream of the previous night. I began to wonder how, in the chaos of postwar Europe, did displaced families manage to reunite? How did a person discover the fate of a loved one? In my mother's case, she had witnesses whom she linked up with in Krakow after the war who attested to her family members' fate. What about families who had no such witnesses, how did they find out what happened to their loved ones? I decided to call my mother in Detroit to see if she could enlighten me on the subject. Currently, it was four in the morning in Detroit; I would have to wait until after my interview with the Polish magazine reporters.

I met the reporters and a cameraman at 11:00 a.m. in the lobby of the Marriott as was previously arranged. I gave a two-hour interview in which I recounted the story of how my acquisition of a Mercury Head dime led to the sequence of events which ultimately brought me to Warsaw for this interview today. One of the reporters suggested that it was divine will that I received the dime which has led to the resurrection of the memory of my father's destroyed family. As of today, they are no longer forgotten: these girls' pictures will soon be seen all over Poland; not only in their magazine but the *Lodz Gazette* as well, as soon as Joanna finishes her story.

It was unfortunate, he said, that I didn't know their names or ages to go along with the pictures. I felt the same way; I needed to somehow find this information. In any event, the reporter said, who cares whose bank the coins are in; what you did to honor the memory of your father's family is priceless.

After the interview, a cameraman accompanying the reporters took several pictures of me and then laid the photos of my father and his sisters on the table in front of us. As he zoomed in to take a picture of the photos, he accidentally knocked over a bottle of Perrier water which I had brought with me. Some of the water ran onto one of the photos. As I grabbed it to wipe off the water, I noticed some very faint printing on the back. There in barely visible, faint blue ink was a stamp: Henri the photographer, 2 Plac Wolnoscie, Lodz.

Holy shit! I thought, there it was, right in front of me all along. I have had these pictures since 1984 and I never noticed this printing: my father's baby pictures are from Lodz. I was dumbfounded. It is amazing how, when one gets so wrapped up in research, he could miss something so obvious.

I thanked the interviewers, said goodbye, and hurried to my room to call my mother. I was anxious to tell her about my dream and find out what she knew about locating family members after the war. Also, I was excited to share the new-found information about the photos of my father's family.

After exchanging telephone greetings with my mother, I quickly got down to business. I told her about my dream and I asked her how my dad knew for sure that all his sisters were killed. My mother asked me if someone hit me over the head in Poland. She said that there was no chance that a sister survived. She explained that my father had witnessed the murders himself and also there were several witnesses who attested to the sisters' murders in the restitution claim. I asked her why one sister's name was left off the deportation list that I had found. My mom explained that after the war she used to be a secretary for the American Joint Distribution Committee in Linz and, even then, lots of mistakes and omissions were made inadvertently.

"Speaking of mistakes," I said, "I have proof that dad was from Lodz. One of the childhood photos of him and his sisters was stamped on the back by a photographer with an address in Lodz. What does that tell you?" I asked.

She replied: "It's obvious what it tells me."

"So you admit you were wrong," I said.

"What wrong?" she protested.

"It obviously tells me that there were no good photographers in Krosno," she added.

I realized I was never going to win an argument with my mother. In fact, no one ever wins an argument with a Jewish mother.

I quickly changed the subject back to post war records and finding family members. My mother responded that in most cases there was no use trying to find somebody, they were likely dead. "If you were the one to survive from the family, chances are, the rest were dead. Nine out of ten Eastern European Jews were killed by the Nazis," she said.

I couldn't argue with her logic, but nevertheless, wanted to know how one went about locating family members. My mother responded that there were two means available after the war. The first was the International Tracing Service which was set up by the office of the Supreme headquarters of the Allied Command and relied on seized German records; you could write them and find out if they had any information about a specific person. Responses were notoriously slow (up to a year) in coming. More effectively, she said, were the American Joint Distribution committee records. These records were compiled by requiring every Jew who found their way into a displaced persons camp or got any assistance from the "Joint" to fill out a card with their name, place of birth, and list their immediate family members, therefore establishing a fairly extensive list of survivors and their families. These records were sent to New York and kept in a central registry. According to my mother, it is unlikely that any Jew who survived the war is not on the registry.

My mother went on to tell me that my dad knew the fates of all his family members except one distant cousin. My father thought that the cousin might have survived, since he escaped to Russia when the war broke out. After the war, however, he was unable to find any information about him and he wasn't on any survivor registries.

I wanted to know a little bit more about my mother's and father's post war history and how she got a job working in Linz for the American Joint Distribution Committee. I asked my mother to continue the story after reuniting with my father in the Berlin train station. She began:

Berlin: 1946

After making their way to the American Joint Distribution Committee displaced persons apartment house at 87 Potsdamer Chaussee, Hirsch, Sally, and her mother Felicja filled out the required survivor registration cards. They were told that they would only be able to be accommodated for a few days. Berlin was being overrun with refugees, the clerk said. Aside from the many Jews fleeing Poland, Berlin was also being flooded with ethnic Germans who had been expelled by the Polish government from the former eastern provinces. The provinces were ceded to Poland as a provision of the international peace agreement. Germans from East Prussia, Silesia, and Pomerania were arriving daily by the train load, the clerk informed them.

Hirsch, still dirty from his all-night trek after jumping from the rail car, was more than happy to leave Berlin as soon as possible. He envisioned that any moment a band of bad tempered Russian policeman would be bursting through the door to arrest him. He told the clerk he needed a meal and a shower and would be ready to leave immediately.

The clerk told them that there was a new displaced persons camp just completed in the Bindermichl section of Linz, Austria, and there was also a large food distribution warehouse located there and it needed workers. Sally would also easily find employment because of her ability to speak English. (Sally was one of the few Polish school girls who studied English as a child).

After making plans to leave the following morning, Sally, Hirsch, and Felicja were given a room for the night. Hirsch was ecstatic that the train would be departing from the suburb of Potsdam so he didn't have to venture though the main Berlin station.

The following morning a nervous Hirsch, along with the rest of the family, boarded the bus to the Potsdam station. He was very relieved when he arrived at the station and saw that the soldiers patrolling the station were wearing white stars on their helmets instead of red ones. (Potsdam was in the American zone of occupation.) The train left Potsdam without incident and arrived in Linz twelve hours later. From the Linz station, Hirsch, Sally, and Felicja took a bus to Bindermichl.

The Bindermichl displaced persons camp was made up of large cement block houses and had a school, kitchen, and numerous workshops. It accommodated 2,500 people. Hirsch was assigned to work in the food warehouse and Sally was sent to work in the camp administration office as a secretary. Felicja mostly stayed at home since she suffered numerous physical ailments. Most problematic were the numerous gallstone attacks. Gallstones are a common complication for people who have subsisted for years on a starvation diet, like that of a concentration camp prisoner.

Sally and Hirsch worked hard at their jobs and also at trying to establish the semblance of a normal married life. It wasn't easy, but they persevered. Sally set up their little apartment in Bindermichl to make it her version of a homey residence. Unlike many of her survivor friends who rushed into motherhood, Sally decided not to have children right away. Instead, she got a dog. He was an adorable Jack Russell Terrier whom she named Jokusz. Sally loved Jokusz and treated him just like he was her baby. He was a pampered dog. Jokusz even got a bath every night. Jokusz was the neighborhood dog. He wandered the halls of Bindermichl and went through the yards. Everyone knew him, loved him, and looked out for him. Life was not so bad in Bindermichl, but it was only a temporary arrangement and was still in Europe, which was not where they wanted their futures to be. Like most displaced Jewish persons in Europe, Hirsch, Sally, and Felicja hoped to immigrate to America, Australia, or Canada. British controlled Palestine was closed to Jewish immigration at that time. They knew that America was their best option, since they already had a relative living there who was willing to sponsor them. With the help of the American Joint Distribution Committee lawyers, they made their application for permanent residence as refugees.

In October 1948 after two years in Bindermichl, Felicja suffered a gallbladder blockage which subsequently ruptured. She was taken to a hospital at the camp and emergency surgery was performed. Two weeks later, on October 31, 1948 she died of septic peritonitis. She was forty-eight years old. The stress of enduring the concentration camps and the anguish of surviving two of her children and husband being murdered had taken its toll, she was prematurely aged. Felicja was buried in the donated Jewish section of the previously mentioned St. Barbara Friedhof cemetery in Linz.

Two weeks later on November 17, 1948, Hirsch and Sally's permanent resident application was approved. Finally, they were coming to America! The much-anticipated departure to America was tinged with sorrow. Sally had to leave behind her beloved dog Jokusz with a neighbor and she had to leave behind the grave of her mother. The mother who carried her through

Warsaw: 2004

After finishing the phone conversation with my mother, I decided to call one of the Polish personal property lawyers in Warsaw which had been recommended to me. I wanted to get some idea of what the legal process might entail.

After telling the lawyer my story, he said that I needed to file an immediate injunction against the Ministry of Culture. Unlike a piece of art which is unique, coins he said, have many duplicates of the same mintage, therefore, a party which is being sued for the coins could easily replace highly valuable uncirculated coins or coins in excellent condition with almost worthless, highly worn coins of the same date. This is especially true if only a list of the coins with no photo evidence of their condition exists. If the coins are in the possession of the Ministry of Culture during a trial and it looks like they might not prevail, this switch can very easily occur, or the coins could disappear altogether.

I suggested that even if an injunction is filed, this could happen anyway, when the ministry was ordered to turn over the coins. The lawyer agreed but thought this is less likely to happen due to the speed of the injunctive process. It would be difficult to find replacements in such short order. It would be much easier during a long-protracted trial.

I was concerned when I heard the words, long and protracted, and asked the lawyer what kind of time frame we might be looking at. He said it could be many months depending on the value of the coins and the persistence of both parties. He went on to tell me that he required a retainer and would also take one third of the value of the coins in a successful action, even though the likelihood of such an outcome was slim. I thanked the lawyer for his time and told him I needed to think things over and I would get back to him.

After I hung up the phone, I thought to myself: do I really want to spend the next several months in a Polish court? I have already spent twenty years looking for these coins. I have proven they were there when everyone scoffed at me; isn't that enough? I have been on the national news on two continents and more importantly, my father and his sisters' images have been seen throughout Europe and North America; what else do I need, and what would happen if and when the case was lost? How would I respond?

I decided I would talk things over with Randi after I got home and go from there. In the meantime, I had seen enough of Poland. My flight was scheduled to leave in the morning; I could hardly wait to get home.

I spent my last night in Warsaw in my room thinking about all that I had seen in my three trips to Poland: Auschwitz-Birkenau, Majdanek, Jedwabne, Lodz, Krakow, and Krosno. What a horrible history this place has, I thought. Did I really want to bring the coins home as a permanent reminder of Poland, or was it time to put this place behind me and move on with my life? I thought about my parents and their lives in Poland and went to bed with a profound sadness. I hate to sound trite and I am not usually an emotional person, but that night, I cried myself to sleep.

In the morning I got a cab and went straight to the airport. As I took my final ride through Warsaw I said to myself; that's it, I am never coming back, I'll deal with the coins from Windsor or not at all, but I'm not coming back here. As the plane took off, I breathed a sigh of relief; I was at peace with my decision.

Windsor:
Spring/Summer, 2004

On my first day home, I had a battery of messages from people who wanted to talk to me: the *Windsor Star* reporter, the local TV news reporter, the CBC national news producer, and a reporter from the *Canadian Sportsman* magazine, which was the national news magazine of the harness racing industry in Canada.

I scheduled a newspaper interview for the following day. The television news producers had picked up some photos and video online and wanted an explanation of why the government was keeping the coins. They ran the story with my explanation that night.

The next day I met the newspaper reporter in my office and did a story about my experience in Poland, and the government's refusal to surrender the coins. Interestingly, the reporter seemed more upset about me coming home empty-handed than I was. In fact, over the next several days, I received calls from all over Canada from people who felt bad that I did not get the coins. Many of them wanted to recommend a good Polish lawyer that they knew who specializes in this type of law. I appreciated their concern and thought; wow, for such a backward country, Poland had a lot of good lawyers.

After I finished with the *Windsor Star* reporter, I called the *Canadian Sportsman* Magazine writer who had left a message for me while I was in Poland. He wanted to do a feature story about me and my twenty-year quest to find my father's coins and in order to put a required horse twist to the story, he also wanted to do a piece on the unusual names of our home raised harness race horses.

One of the fun things about breeding horses is that you get to name them. When we first started in the breeding business, I wanted to have a distinctive theme for all our horses' names. That way, they would immediately be recognized as originating from our farm. Some farms use a farm name as a prefix or suffix in all their horse's names. The Armstrong Brothers Farms, for example, used "Armbro" before every name of a horse that was raised at their farm. I wanted to do something a little different. I chose to name all our horses with World War II or Jewish history themed monikers. It was these names which intrigued the writer at the *Canadian Sportsman*. I scheduled to meet with him at the end of the current week.

In the meantime, I was happy to go back to work as an equine veterinarian. Unfortunately, for the time being, I wasn't going to be able to retire early from the proceeds of the sale of the coins. I really enjoyed the horse business anyway, and didn't mind the ten to twelve-hour days I routinely worked. I started right back with a full schedule of patients two days after returning to Windsor from Poland.

I met with Dave Briggs, the *Canadian Sportsman* writer, in my office as scheduled on Friday May 7, 2004. After a four-hour interview in which I retold the saga of the coins and my travels through Poland, Dave removed a computer printout from his briefcase listing the horses bred by the Biederman farm. "Tell me about the origin and meaning of these names," he enquired. He started with the most obvious horse on the list: Zeglarska Street.

In 2003, after learning of my father's Lodz home address from Izzy Oliwek, I decided that I would name the next foal Zeglarska Street. There were already a couple superstar harness racehorses with "Street" in their name. There was Vine Street and Bond Street for example, so I thought why not a Zeglarska Street? When I did the interview with Dave Briggs, Zeglarska Street was a yearling and had not yet started her race training.

Coincidently, or maybe not, some say it was pre-ordained, Zeglarska Street turned out to be the best horse we ever raised on the farm. Of the approximately 2,000 filly pacers born each year in Ontario, only the top ten are good enough to race in the Ontario sire stakes Gold Series as two and three-year-olds. The Gold Series features five races a year which offer a purse of 165,000 dollars each. The odds of breeding a horse that will be competitive in the Gold Series are about two hundred to one. The odds of breeding a Gold Series winner are even smaller. For a small breeder, like we were, who bred six mares a year, having a gold winner is quite an accomplishment. Zeglarska Street won two Gold Series races in her career. She was the only Gold winner we ever produced.

The next horse on the list was Mila Eighteen. 18 Mila Street was the street address of the Zionist Fighting Organization headquarters in the Warsaw Ghetto. *Mila 18* was also the title of a novel by Leon Uris about the Warsaw Ghetto Uprising. To this day, the book continues to be one of my favorite historical novels of all time. As I mentioned earlier, I visited the site of the underground bunker at 18 Mila Street when I was in Warsaw. Today, a monument sits atop the rubble pile that is the destroyed remains of the headquarters.

Mila Eighteen raced with moderate success at the lesser levels (known as the Grass Roots) of the Ontario sires stakes at two and three years old. During her three-year-old season, she injured a knee and was retired.

Zydowska was the next name on the list. The Polish pronunciation is Zhi-dove-skah. The name literally means "Jewish" in the Polish language. When Randi and I first started traveling in Poland we would always hear people whisper and then nudge each other with the warning: "Zydowska: they are Jews," take appropriate precautions. We would hear this term when we walked into a city hall searching for vital records or when checking into a hotel or even on the street, especially in Lodz. Come to think of it, it wasn't all that uncommon in the Krosno vernacular, either. Randi and I started calling each other Zydowska for her, the feminine adjective, and Zydowski for me, the masculine form. In Poland, they became our pet names for one another. I decided that the next foal after Zeglarska Street was going to named Zydowska or Zydowski, depending on whether it was a colt or a filly. I have previously mentioned that as the son of two Holocaust survivors I have some mental problems. I do, however, have a sense of humor, twisted as it may be.

Zydowska injured a tendon as a yearling, during training and only raced a few times. She never won a race. Let's face it; there aren't a lot of great Jewish athletes anyway.

The next horse on Dave's list was named Stalingrad. We bought Stalingrad's mother, Vodka on Ice, when she was pregnant with Stalingrad. The previous owner had already set a precedent by naming Vodka on Ice's foals with Russian themed names. Stalingrad was obviously named after the city where the infamous battle occurred that was considered the turning point of World War II.

Stalingrad the horse was born with an airway abnormality and never raced. It was a waste of a great name.

The next Russian front name I came up with was Katyusha Rocket. This horse was sired by a stallion named Pacific Rocket, so I thought the name Katyusha Rocket was appropriate. A Katyusha Rocket was a Russian artillery weapon which struck fear into the German forces. My father's Russian friend, who showed me his box of military medals when I was a boy, was a Katyusha Rocket artillery man.

Unfortunately, Katyusha Rocket the horse suffered a large colon torsion as a yearling and died.

The final Russian front themed horse name was Not One Step Back. It was the English translation of Supreme Commander Josef Stalin's order number 227: "Nie shagu nazad." This was an order to the Red Army to stand

and fight; retreating was no longer an option under any circumstances. Not One Step Back became the rallying cry of the Red Army throughout the remainder of the war. We had a partner on this horse who wanted to sell him rather than go through the expense of training and therefore we sold him as a yearling.

Unfortunately, Not One Step Back took a giant leap back when he broke a bone in his foot and was retired before making it to the races. He was later donated, by his new owners, to a therapeutic riding stable for the handicapped.

After all the bad luck with the horses that had Russian front themed names, I discontinued this line of naming. It seemed to be a good idea.

The final two horses on Dave's list were Golda Meihorse and Ben Netanyahorse. These two names were word plays on the Israeli Prime Ministers Golda Meir and Benjamin Netanyahu. Both of these horses had moderate success at the racetrack. Neither of them were leaders at the finish line very often.

Our experience with breeding horses was actually quite typical. Some of the young horses do not make it into training; they get sick or injured and are prematurely retired. Many other horses who begin training do not make it to the races and the ones who do are often not that successful. It is extremely rare to get a superstar racehorse. Horse breeding is a tough game and an expensive one. It was ironic, I thought, that Zeglarska Street was our best horse, ever.

After I concluded the interview with Dave Briggs, he made an appointment for a photographer to come to the farm to take some photographs of me and the horses. The article was scheduled to appear in the next issue of the *Canadian Sportsman*.

The *Canadian Sportsman* photographer arrived on the following Monday. He said that he needed three types of photos to be included in the story. One was a picture of me with my notes and records and books demonstrating all the research that I had done. The second was a picture of me with the horse, Zeglarska Street. Lastly, he wanted old pre-war photographs of my father and his family. When telling the story of the Holocaust, there is no image more powerful than pre-war family photos. Here in these photos were adorable, smiling, happy children who would, in a few short years, be murdered.

Like the Polish magazine photographer before him, the *Canadian Sportsman* photographer took close up pictures of my father's childhood photos with his mother and three sisters. Inevitably, he asked the obvious question: "What were the girls' names and how old were they when they were killed?" These questions reinforced for me the need to find this information, since I still did not have the answers.

After the photographer left, I was bothered by my lack of knowledge about my father's sisters so I went on line and wrote to the International Tracing Service, Document Search Department to request information on immediate family members of Hirsch Biederman born in 1925 in Lodz, Poland. It was not possible (and still is not today) to do an online search of all the documents in their collections yourself; the request for information had to be sent to them and then their staff would do an in house search of the millions of documents. When they were completed, the results would be forwarded to the person making the inquiry.

The International Tracing Service had been located in Frankfurt, Germany. It was a center for documentation, information, and research on Nazi persecution and the Holocaust. The organization was originally set up by the headquarters of the Allied Forces in 1943 as a tracing service for missing persons. In 1947, the tracing service was taken over by the International Refugee Organization. When the occupation of Germany was ended, the Tracing Service was turned over to the International Red Cross but was funded by the Federal Republic of Germany. The International Tracing Service was not without controversy. Much like the Polish authorities, whether or not inquiries were answered was often at the whim or discretion of whomever happened to be working at the time that the inquiry was made. In 2007, after worldwide criticism, the International Tracing Service finally bowed to the pressure and opened their archives to the public. The newly opened archives are located in Bad Arolsen, Germany and can now be personally visited, but only with a previously scheduled appointment.

I had previously sent letters to the International Tracing Service enquiring about my father in the 1980s when I had also sent letters to Krosno. After about a year, I received a letter in response saying that there were no records which matched my search parameters. In 2004, the World Wide Web was still in its relative infancy, and new records were being computerized and added to databases around the world daily. I hoped to find out something new about my father and his sisters. Unfortunately, my inquiry did not yield any information about my father's sisters and I only received information about him that I already knew.

At the same time that I sent a request to the International Tracing Service, I also sent the identical request for information to the United States Holocaust Museum Document Search Department in Washington, DC. Their response came very swiftly. After approximately two weeks from the day my request was sent to the museum, I received an email titled:

"Congratulations: your search returned four matches." I excitedly opened the email thinking, once and for all, I would have my answers about my father's sisters' names and birthdates. The following is an excerpt of the email:

Congratulations, your search returned four records for 'immediate family members of Hirsch Biederman':

Harry Biederman
Sally Biederman
Edward Biederman
Mark Biederman, born Detroit, MI, 1961"

I learned that the Holocaust Museum kept up to date records on survivors! I imagine that there are researchers who might find this post war, current information valuable. From my perspective, I wanted to smash my computer to pieces, but I decided against it; I still might need it in the future.

The following day I received the *Canadian Sportsman* in the mail. I was featured on the cover and there was an impressive six-page story inside. The article featured maps tracing my father's movements through Europe, and then, my following of his trail half a century later; ultimately leading to the discovery of the coin collection. My father and his sisters' pictures were also prominently displayed in the magazine. This was the third major publication in a month to feature these photos. If nothing else came from the coin quest, I thought, I certainly have educated a lot of people about the Holocaust. My father's family was the ultimate illustration of the tragic human toll; without names and faces, six million murders are just a statistic.

Over the next few days as I began settling back into my routine of being an equine veterinarian, I received a call from a television production company from Montreal called Bleu, Blanc et Rouge Productions. They were the producers of a show called "Past Lives" which aired on the Canadian Global TV network. *Past Lives* was a show that featured ordinary people who, when doing genealogical research, found something extraordinary in their family background. The producers thought that my story would be perfect for their show. They wanted to send a production team to Windsor and spend a week filming me in order to gather enough footage to put together an episode. They were planning on following me through a typical week and have me talk about my life, my research, and my family history.

At first, I was reluctant to agree to do a TV episode. I wondered what they wanted with me. What was so unusual about a Jewish boy from Detroit, the son of two Holocaust survivors, one of whom was on Schindler's List, who became a horse veterinarian and breeder and went on to find gold coins buried for sixty-five years in Lodz, Poland?

I was also concerned about having television cameras around my horse clinic for a week. Horse people, especially racehorse people, are very distrustful of outsiders. Most of them are uncomfortable with answering a lot of questions about their horses and prefer to keep to themselves. I didn't think any of my clients would be comfortable having cameras filming us diagnosing and treating their horses. In the end, I did agree to do the show but told the producers that they would have to turn off the cameras if anyone of my clients felt uncomfortable or objected to being filmed.

The filming was scheduled to take place the week of August 9, 2004. That day, which was a Monday, the production team arrived from Montreal. It included a director, a cameraman and a sound technician. The first day was spent on introductions and then planning the shooting schedule for the week. The shooting was scheduled to begin Tuesday, August 10. Coincidently, August 10 was the thirtieth anniversary of my Bar Mitzvah and the sixty-second anniversary of that dark day in Krosno when my father's entire family was killed. We spent the morning shooting a few horse appointments, and then in the afternoon I went and bought five Yahrtzeit (memorial) candles, one for each of my father's murdered family members. We set the lit candles alongside pictures of my father's family, on the kitchen table for the cameraman to film. It made for a very touching scene. Afterward, we went to the synagogue (where I was the president) and I was filmed saying the memorial prayer for the dead and the one for the murdered victims of the Holocaust. That concluded the first day of filming. Surprisingly, all my horse clients were very amenable to being filmed that morning; a lot of them actually enjoyed it.

The morning of the second day of filming was spent much like the first, shooting horse appointments and an arthroscopic surgery. I was thinking that aside from the genealogy stuff there was material for a great reality show: Racehorse Hospital. The focus of the second day was how I got interested in the horses and we spent a lot of time on camera discussing my background. When I was in high school my father would go to the race track three to four nights a week; often he would take me with him. At first, I really didn't have an interest in the horses themselves, I was more interested in the handicapping and also just hanging out with my dad. Unlike my father, I had no interest in gambling. In fact, I hated to gamble but I loved mathematics and figures. I loved numerical puzzles. For me, the joy of the race track was trying to put together a mathematical formula using past performance data to predict the likely winner of the race. After the third race of the evening, the tracks would sell the program for the next night of racing. I would usually have my father buy me one and I would take it to school the next day and handicap that evening's races. I kept the program tucked inside my school book to keep it out of sight of the teacher. It appeared to the teacher that I was one of the most avid, interested students in the material; little did they know that I was reading and handicapping the horse program. In reality, I don't think I ever read one word of my school textbooks. I was actually fairly successful at picking the winner of each race. I found two variables in the past performance lines, which were most correlated with winning or losing. If a horse led by a wide margin in these two variables there was an 85 to 90 percent chance it would win the race. A broader explanation of this will be in my next book: *How to Win at the Horse Races*.

We then began to discuss how I became a horse veterinarian. Originally, I wanted to be a small animal veterinarian. As a kid, I was a bit of a loner and was more attached to my pets than to people. Psychologists will tell you that this is not unusual for a child of Holocaust survivors. They claim we have trouble establishing normal relationships and trusting other people. After my first dog died, I was devastated and I decided I was going to be a veterinarian. During high school, I volunteered one day at a small animal clinic. I hated it. While the medicine cases were interesting, most of the day was spent doing elective surgery (spays, castrations, cat declaws, etc.) on otherwise healthy animals. This was not for me. One of my father's friends who owned racehorses suggested I volunteer at the track for a horse veterinarian. I did and immediately loved it. The horse backstretch is a whole different world than I had ever experienced. Aside from working with the horses, I loved interacting with all the interesting characters one finds at a racetrack. After a couple days of volunteering, I had decided: I was going to be a horse veterinarian.

The second night of filming was spent at Windsor Raceway. The crew was given rare unlimited access and got some great behind the scenes shots. The best one was when the cameraman was able to ride in the starting car for one of the races. In harness racing the starting gate is mobile and is basically a modified sedan with two folding wings to keep the horses in line. The car has a driver and a starter. The driver drives the car and faces forward; the starter sits in a modified hutch and faces rearward towards the horses. At the starting line the driver accelerates and drives off as the starter pulls a lever and folds in the wings. I have been driven in the starting car many times and have sat in the starter's hutch. Believe me, there is no more awesome and impressive sight than seeing ten, one thousand pound excited beasts coming right at you at forty miles an hour, while ten humans in a cart strapped to their back are attempting to control them with nothing more than a couple leather strings attached to a six ounce piece of metal in their mouths. This film clip ended up being the opening scene in my episode.

During the third day of filming, the director planned on having me do an on-camera interview discussing the progression of my research from the day I decided to look for the coins, until the day they were found. They thought it was amazing that I started with nothing more than an idea of finding family coins somewhere in Poland to actually unearthing them twenty years later. They wanted to know how I did it. This was, after all, a genealogy show. I must say that as I relived the events, I was amazed myself at the incredible coincidences that occurred which allowed me to succeed.

Firstly, I felt it was important to make the film crew aware of the obstacle that the Jewish genealogist researching in Eastern European countries encounters, especially in Poland. The pervasive anti-Semitism of the officials controlling the availability of information from the archives made it difficult to acquire any records, even if they existed. I believed all along that some records did still indeed exist in the Polish hometowns of many of my family members. Because the Jewish genealogist was unlikely to get any cooperation from the authorities in these towns, he or she had to find other means of obtaining information. I doubt, on the other hand, that if an Irish person, for example, went back to his or her father's hometown in Ireland, he or she would face any obstacles whatsoever in obtaining whatever records they desired. Sadly, dealing with the recalcitrant officials was a sad fact of life that had to be faced in dealing with research in Poland.

In my case though, I still had to correctly find out where in Poland was my father's hometown, before I could even worry about obtaining records.

To launch my quest, the most significant thing that happened was the release of the movie *Schindler's List*. If not for this movie, I doubt that all the interest in Jewish, Polish genealogy, which served as a catalyst for the starting of the websites which were so helpful to me, would have come about. What is even more shocking is that my father was on Schindler's List and I didn't even know it. It wasn't until a horse trainer client happened to catch his name on the list as it was scanned during the movie, that I learned my father's inclusion. I had seen the movie multiple times and never noticed it myself.

Finding Albert White was also an incredible stroke of luck for me. What were the chances that another Jew from the Krosno airbase of whom there were only about one hundred, and who knew my dad, would be on a fledgling Jewish Genealogy website? If not for Albert White, I still might be hanging around the Krosno city hall, trying to get some information.

Another incredible stroke of luck was finding a Lodz native (Izzy Oliwek) who happened to have been my father's neighbor. I found it incredible that my mother would have a chance meeting with him in a restaurant in Florida and just in time; he died a few months after I spoke with him. I myself had no luck finding anyone else from Lodz who knew him despite spending hours researching the available archives and records.

We had to conclude the interview when it was time for me to leave for my men's league hockey game. I have been a goaltender and a hockey fanatic, since I was about nine years old. Interestingly, my mother told me that her brother Henryk, who was beaten to death by the Nazis in the Krakow Ghetto, was a highly regarded Polish hockey player. He had to quit his team when the Germans invaded Poland and immediately barred Jews from playing organized sports. In all my years of playing minor hockey as a youth, my mother never came to any of my games. I guess it was too painful for her to watch me play since it would bring back the memories of her slain brother. This was unfortunate for me and was another example of how the Holocaust affected my life.

Friday morning was the final day of shooting for the *Past Lives* show. For that day, the director planned on doing a virtual tour of the sites which we had talked about during the previous days. He asked me to produce all of my photo albums from my trips to Europe and Poland. We spent the day going through pictures of each location and then the cameraman would take a shot of the ones the director selected, while I explained where each photo was taken and described the significance of every pictured place. The director continued to be intrigued with the August 10 story about my Bar Mitzvah being on the same day as the anniversary of the murder of my father's entire family. He asked me if I had any photos from that day. I responded that of course I did, every Bar Mitzvah party had a professional photographer. I scrambled to locate my Bar Mitzvah album which I probably had not looked at since I showed it to Randi shortly after our engagement seven years previously. It was probably an additional twenty years since I saw it prior to that. After I finally found it, I realized that this would be the first time I had seen the album since I learned of the coincidental date of the murder of my father's family. As I opened the album, the first picture was a family portrait with me alongside my parents and my brother. I now saw this picture in a completely different light. This was the first time I viewed my father's face with the knowledge of what he was going through that day. It was very unsettling. I never noticed it before, but the pain in that face was very evident. I can't believe he kept his secret inside. How could he not tell anyone? I wished he were alive so I could talk to him. A range of emotions went through me. I had to take a break and went to the kitchen for a bottle of water.

As I was in the kitchen sipping water, I began to ponder. I lost my father to pancreatic cancer when I was nineteen years old. That was the most difficult day of my life. I didn't know how to move forward. I still had a mother, a brother, a home, and my father left a decent inheritance so that I would be able to continue my college career all the way through veterinary school. But even with all that, I was devastated. Now I'm looking at my father wondering how in the hell did he survive? How did he do it? His parents and sisters were all murdered on the same day, one month before his seventeenth birthday. He had no one left. He had no home. He had no money. Additionally, he had no time to mourn. Had he not gotten up the following morning at the 5:00 a.m. reveille and been ready to put in a full day's work, he probably would have been shot. How did he do it? How could he have gone to his grave without talking to me? "Why didn't you tell me?" I began to sob. "Why didn't you tell me!?"

I somehow managed to collect myself, and we finished shooting for the episode with the Bar Mitzvah pictures. The crew then packed up, and I saw them off to the airport. They told me that they thought this story would make their best episode to date and would likely be the first show of the new season. I was looking forward to seeing it in September.

A few days after the *Past Lives* team left, I began to again think about what could have motivated my father to go on and survive after the murder of his entire family. Surely something must have driven him to keep going through the many more years of misery that lay ahead of him. I started to ask this question of the many survivors that I knew. Many of them gave the same response: "I had to survive for my brother," or "my sister"; "They needed me, there was no one else." This answer obviously did not apply to my father; he had no one else to live for. Other survivors said: "I had to survive to bear witness for what had happened, because in future generations no one would believe it." That seemed like a fine answer, but I didn't think that it would be a strong enough motivation for my father. There had to be something else!

Some years later, when I was in Israel, I was introduced to a Holocaust survivor who was a member of the Nakamah group. "Nakamah" means "revenge" in Hebrew and the Nakamah group was comprised of Holocaust survivors who hunted down and killed SS Nazis, who were responsible for mass Jewish murder, after the war. This man was about the same age as my father and also had his entire family killed when he was a teenager. When I asked him how he found the motivation to survive the concentration camps he answered: "That's easy, one word: revenge." He had to survive, he said, because he was going to hunt down and kill the bastard who was responsible for the deaths of his entire family. Every day that went by and the more deprivation he suffered, the stronger his will to survive became.

After I heard this, a lightbulb clicked on in my brain. That's it! That's my father! I began to think that maybe that's the reason for my father's mysterious and unexplained appearance in Austria in August of 1945. Earlier, I had pondered what could have been the reason for my father to delay his attempt to retrieve the coins. What could have been more important? The answer now seemed obvious: Nakamah!

In order to validate my hypothesis, I needed to find out the origins of the SS men who were responsible for the killing of the Jews, including my father's mother and two eldest sisters, in Krosno on August 10, 1942. If they were from Linz or the surrounding areas of Austria, I would feel that there was a strong likelihood that the reason my father went to Austria after the war, was to try to locate these murderers.

But first I had to find out if my mother knew the reason for my father being in Linz in August 1945. When I questioned her and told her of my theory for him going there, I expected her to tell me that I was crazy and there was no way that happened. Instead I got quite the opposite response. She said she thought that my father, indeed, at some point mentioned that he did try to find the people responsible for killing his mother. She, however, thought he went back to Krosno after the war to look for the killers. When I described his unexplained presence in Linz, she was intrigued although not necessarily ready to agree with my theory. I also argued that it was unlikely that any of the SS men were still in Poland after the war and it would be even less likely for them to have remained in Krosno, where they would risk being recognized by the remaining Jews. They would then be readily pointed out to the Soviet authorities. It was much more likely that they would have returned home, especially if that home was in American occupied territory. No SS man wanted to remain in Russian held territory and later risk falling into the hands of the Russians. They would then have to trust their fate to the Soviet system of justice. This, for most SS men meant summary execution.

Although there were a lot of SS men mentioned in relation to the Krosno massacre, it was difficult for me to determine who was mostly responsible for the murders of my father's mother and two sisters. There was not a lot of information about these men or their nationalities in the historical records that I was able to find. Albert White, who was a witness, also didn't remember many specifics about them. There was however, some revealing information I did know.

The plan to exterminate the majority of the Jews of the General Government region of Poland (of which Krosno was part) was named Operation Reinhard in honor of Reinhard Heydrich, a top Nazi official who was assassinated by Czech commandos in Prague in July 1942. How sick, by the way, is an ideology that honors someone by naming a plan to murder 2.5 million men, women and children after them? Heydrich was the man who chaired the Wannsee Conference in January 1942, which was the meeting held to inform and elicit support from various leaders within the Nazi government regarding the "final solution."

The three top deputies in Poland who oversaw the execution of Operation Reinhard were all Austrian Nazis coordinating operations from Lublin. The man in charge of the operation was named Odilo Globocnik, he oversaw the establishment of the Belzec, Sobibor, and Treblinka death camps in the General Government as well as organized many of the round ups and transportation of Jews to these camps. Globocnik's top assistant was named Hermann Hofle, a fellow Austrian who was also an active participant in the deportation of the General Government Jews to the death camps. Globocnik's next in command was Ernst Lerch who also organized mass shootings of Jews in the Lublin district.

After the war, these three men fled Poland and were discovered hiding out in an Alpine mountain hut on Lake Weissensee, Austria 190 miles from Linz. After they were surrounded by a British army unit, Globocnik immediately committed suicide by biting down on a cyanide capsule; Hofle and Lerch were then arrested. After a short time in custody, both men were released. Hofle was again arrested in Austria in 1961 by a newly appointed war crimes commission but hung himself in his cell before his trial began. Lerch died in 1997, a free man.

The significance of the backgrounds of these three men, for me, is that it demonstrates a distinct Austrian connection to the General Government Nazi apparatus. The underlings who committed the Krosno murders could have very likely been previous Austrian cronies who were appointed to their positions by these men.

When I take this into consideration, along with my father's unknown whereabouts for three months (he was liberated in the Czech Republic on May 8, 1945 from Schindler's factory and was off the radar until he turned up at Mauthausen near Linz on August 6, 1945), I believe there is a possibility he went to Austria in an attempt to avenge his family's murder. Unfortunately, this remains speculation and is another of my many lingering unanswered questions. I have also read conspiracy theories which claim Globocnik was murdered by Jewish avengers and the official British army report of suicide was falsified to cover for them. Most respected historians do not give any credibility to the conspiracy theorists, but who knows?

It was two weeks since the *Past Lives* film crew had left, and I was settling back into my normal routine when I received an unexpected phone call. The coins, meanwhile, were safely stowed in the Lodz Museum of Ethnography and Archaeology. I didn't make any inquiries about them so as not to give the Poles a heads up, no pun intended, that I was going to attempt to reclaim them. I worried that if I took any action, as the lawyer in Warsaw suggested, that they would promptly disappear. The caller was from Montreal and was the chief of production for the *Past Lives* television show. I was gratified when he told me that he thought my episode was too important and too valuable to use photos instead of live shots in Poland. He then asked me the dreaded question: would I be willing to return to Lodz to do additional filming for the show?

Oh no, I thought to myself, not again! I was just there and if I recall, I said that I was *never* going back. Never does not mean six months! I told Brian (the producer) that I would have to give it some thought. He said that if I decided to go, he was planning on a trip in the first week in October.

Aside from the fact that I hated Poland, October was a terrible time for me to be away from my practice. Our local racetrack, Windsor Raceway, closes for the summer and then reopens for a new season beginning in October. It is really important for a veterinarian to be on hand for the large influx of horses to the area that accompanies the opening of the track for a new horse racing season. Beside the inevitable rash of sick horses which occurs after inter mixing them from all different locations; it is also important for me to meet the new trainers that invariably come to Windsor at the start of every racing season. I told Brian that I really didn't think it was a good time to go.

He asked me if I would consider it for a few days and call him back. I said that I would. He said that although their budget only allowed them to offer me a small per diem, all my other expenses would be covered. "Think of it as an all-expenses paid vacation, how often does an opportunity like that come along?" he asked.

I told him that an October in Lodz, Poland is not exactly anyone's idea of a dream vacation. In fact, a week in Lodz is more like a sentence than a vacation.

As I promised Brian I would, I spent a few days talking it over with Randi and ended up deciding to go. We figured I could survive one week there and my father's story would be much more meaningful if the show was actually shot in Poland. When I called Brian to let him know of my decision to go, he was ecstatic. He said he would put together an itinerary and contact me in a few days.

A few days later, I received an email from Brian with our itinerary for the trip to Poland. I was scheduled to fly out of Detroit on October 9 and after a stop in Frankfurt, Germany, arrive in Warsaw in the morning of October 10. In Warsaw, I was to meet the television crew which consisted of a director, producer, soundman and cameraman and our guide and driver Derek. We would then proceed directly to Lodz for three days of filming and then onto the Gross-Rosen Concentration Camp near Wroclaw for the last day of shooting. I was then scheduled to spend the final night in Wroclaw and fly out on the morning of the fourteenth, and after a couple of stops, arrive back in Detroit that evening.

Although my father, along with the rest of the Schindler Jews only spent a short time at Gross-Rosen, the director thought it was important for any Holocaust story to include a concentration camp in the filming. When the Schindler Jews were evacuated from Schindler's factory in Krakow/Plaszow to be transferred to his new factory in Brunnlitz, it wasn't completely finished. Consequently, they had to stop in Gross-Rosen, where they stayed for one week, until the Brunnlitz camp was ready.

Because of my anticipated one-week absence from the clinic in October, we heavily booked our appointment schedule in September. By the time October 9 came around, I was exhausted and needed a break. It would have been nice if my father buried some coins in Hawaii instead of Poland, I thought.

Before I left for Poland I called Joanna Podolska at the *Lodz Gazette* to let her know that I would be arriving with a film crew in a few days. She said my story had still been garnering a lot of interest and asked if it would be okay if one of their reporters accompanied me and the film crew around Lodz. I told her I would be fine with that and I would let her know if the *Past Lives* producer had any objections. When I notified Brian that there may be a Polish reporter with us he saw no problem with it and, in fact, was excited about the publicity. I'm guessing he was hoping to sell the episode in Europe.

Lodz: October 2004

I departed Detroit on Saturday, October 9 at 6:00 p.m. and arrived without incident in Warsaw on Sunday the tenth at 10:00 a.m. I met Derek the guide right at the gate as I got off the plane. He was holding up a sign saying "Past Lives." Derek was a lot younger than my previous Warsaw guide, Mishkel, and seemed a lot friendlier. I didn't sense any anti-Semitic feelings from him whatsoever. Derek and I got to know each other while waiting for the television crew to land at the airport; they arrived about an hour and a half after me. To my surprise it was a completely different group than the crew who came to Windsor. The crew consisted of a production coordinator named Karen, a director named Rohan, a cameraman named Peter, and the soundman was named Christian. After exchanging greetings with the crew we went through Customs. It took a couple of hours to clear all their equipment. Finally at 2:00 p.m., we got in Derek's van and headed for Lodz. I was a little nervous about spending three days there. In the previous two trips, I only stayed for a total of one night. Derek and the new TV crew seemed like a pretty fun loving bunch so I figured I would try to enjoy myself on this excursion.

After an hour and a half drive we arrived in Lodz and made our first stop at the main Jewish cemetery. It was located at the intersection of the two major highways entering downtown Lodz from the east. This location would end up having important historical significance. When it was completed in 1892, the Lodz Jewish cemetery was the largest cemetery in the world. Today, it is still one of the largest Jewish cemeteries in the world and is the largest in Europe. It contains over 200,000 separate marked graves, although most of the headstones have been vandalized or destroyed, and another approximately 50,000 bodies in a mass grave who were the victims of the Lodz Ghetto.

To my surprise, as opposed to the abandoned Jewish cemeteries in Linz and Krosno, the Lodz cemetery was still operational and had a functioning archive as well as a maintenance crew. Although the cemetery suffered heavy damage over the years, currently, the grounds were actually fairly well kept. Apparently the cemetery is being duly supported by the Lodz historical society and Jewish organizations around the world.

Since *Past Lives* was a genealogy show, Rohan the director wanted to check the archives and see if we could find the graves of any of my ancestors. The archival office was fully computerized and had a staff of three people. There were a few Biedermans listed in the archives, but one name in particular caught my attention: Saul Biederman who died on January 21, 1939. My father also died on a January 21! I wondered if this was his grandfather. When examining the record further, I noticed it said: Saul son of Hirsch. I knew right away that this had to be my great grandfather! In Jewish tradition, graves are inscribed with a person's Hebrew name. Every Hebrew name uses the patronymic "son of" or "daughter of" after a person's first name. Another Jewish tradition is to name a newborn after the most recent deceased ancestor. Since my father's grandfather, and my great grandfather, Saul was still alive in 1925 when my father was born, Saul's father, Hirsch would have been that person whom my father was named after.

Rohan thought that these traditions made for very interesting genealogy and was pleasantly surprised that we actually had success in finding an ancestor. I wondered if there were any records of next of kin living at 7 Zeglarska Street. I thought a record like that would go a long way in helping my coin case. Unfortunately, the archives only had the name of the deceased with no further family information. I was disappointed after my initial excitement of finding Saul that I couldn't find documentation of the Biederman family address.

We were then given a section number, row, and grave number for Saul, "son of Hirsch" Biederman. The Lodz cemetery was arranged in a grid of 160 numbered sections consisting of twenty-five rows of forty graves each. A cemetery worker offered to take us to the site. Before going to visit Saul's grave, I quickly ran across the street to a local floral shop and purchased eight roses to place on the headstone; six for each member of my father's immediate family and two for myself and Randi. Even though Randi did not accompany me on this trip, she was with me through many difficult treks through Poland in the past and deserved to be represented.

Unfortunately, when we got to Saul's section at the far back corner of cemetery the graves were unrecognizable. What the Nazis and the vandals didn't demolish, nature did. Much of the cemetery was in the process of undergoing uncontrolled natural reforestation and the sprouting trees had knocked over the few remaining headstones and obliterated the architecture of many sections. In Saul's particular section, there was almost no way to determine where each row and grave number was located among the newly sprouted forest. I walked to the approximate area where I estimated row twelve, grave twenty-three would have been and left the flowers. I said a traditional Jewish blessing when visiting a gravesite and was grateful that Saul died in January of 1939, eight months before the Nazis invaded Poland. Thankfully he wasn't subjected to the upcoming horror known as the Holocaust. As I thought about Saul's and my father's coincidental mortality date, even though I'm not superstitious or into numerology, it was a little uncanny to me how certain dates kept repeating.

As we walked back to the main gate, I noticed several deep trenches dug along the periphery of the cemetery. I asked the guide if there was any purpose to these ditches. Derek looked at me and asked, "You don't know the story?" "No, I don't," I responded. He went on to explain that in January 1945, Hans Biebow the corrupt, ruthless Nazi administrator of the Lodz Ghetto, after learning that the Red Army was ten kilometers from Lodz, ordered the remaining Jewish population killed. By this time, there were only approximately nine hundred Jews left alive in the ghetto. A group of these remaining Jews were ordered to the cemetery and told to begin digging these trenches which were to become mass graves. A mass execution after forcing the victims to dig their own graves was a common occurrence in many places during the Holocaust. On the morning of January 19, as the remaining Jews were being marched to the cemetery, the cadence of the SS men was disrupted by the distinctive, deafening rumble of Soviet made twelve-cylinder diesel engines heading directly for the cemetery. A frightened German soldier, who had moments earlier abandoned the front line, ran by yelling: "Run for your lives, the Russians are coming!" Seconds later, the lead fifty-ton heavily armored ISU 122mm Soviet mobile assault cannon of the First Guards Tank Army came into view. The terrified SS men dropped their weapons, some shit their pants, and they all high tailed it west. The 877 remaining Jews of the Lodz Ghetto had been liberated by the Red Army. Fortunately, for them, the cemetery was situated directly in the path of the Soviet advance at those eastern approaches to the city, mentioned earlier.

Hans Biebow, the aforementioned Nazi administrator of the ghetto, was able to escape Lodz and return to his hometown of Bremen, Germany. After the war, he was recognized in Bremen by a survivor of the Lodz Ghetto and was then arrested by the Allied War Crimes Commission. In 1947 he was extradited to Lodz where he stood trial from April 23 to April 30. He was found guilty on all of the multiple counts of war crimes and crimes against humanity that he was charged with and executed by hanging on June 23, 1947.

When we left the cemetery, we all piled into Derek's van, along with all the equipment, and went to check in at our hotel for a short rest before dinner. We were booked to stay at the Ibis hotel which was just south of downtown Lodz. The Ibis hotel was only a couple of years old and I was pleasantly surprised at how clean and comfortable, albeit very utilitarian, it was. It was very similar to a Quality Inn in the United States, and the staff was very pleasant. When I went to check in and pick up my key, nary a disparaging whisper of "Zydowski" was heard. Was this the Lodz I had come to know?

After the entire crew also checked in, we agreed to meet back in the lobby in an hour where Derek would meet us and take us to dinner. I went up to my room and changed and decided to go for a short walk before meeting the crew for dinner. By this time, nightfall had begun to descend on Lodz and the temperatures dropped to near freezing. I was totally unprepared for how cold it was in Lodz. I packed mostly short sleeve shirts and I only brought one light fall jacket. I instantly began to think of all the pictures of Auschwitz I had seen that were taken in the fall months. The prisoners were only wearing light wool pants, a wool shirt and most had wooden shoes with no socks. Here I was healthy and well fed and couldn't handle the cold. How did these half-starved, emaciated beings survive the frigid weather? Fortunately for me, there was a new modern shopping mall called the Galleria right next to the hotel. I went in and bought a wool sweater at one of the stores. Surprisingly, the quality of the mall was actually on par with that of a modern American one.

Sporting my new sweater, I went back to the hotel and rendezvoused with the crew and Derek and then we went to dinner. We went to an Italian restaurant on the newly refurbished, fairly fashionable Piotrkowska Street. I ate the customary vegetarian pizza. I don't trust the safety of the meat in foreign countries. After dinner, Rohan wanted to get some night shots of me in some of the historic places of Lodz. The entire crew was Montreal based and brought winter coats, hats and gloves. I guess they expected frigid first weeks in October. I was expecting seventy-degree weather like we had in Detroit before I left for Poland. After walking around Lodz at night for an hour in ever dropping temperatures, my hands and feet were completely numb. I was happy when we finally called it quits for the evening. Frigid October weather also had a significant impact on my father sixty years previously, when he arrived in Gross-Rosen. When we returned to the hotel, Karen, the production coordinator relayed the schedule for the next day's shooting before we went to our rooms. The production team arranged for us to tour the Museum of Archaeology and Ethnography at 11 a.m. and also see the coin collection. At the museum, we were also scheduled to meet with Joanna Podolska and the *Lodz Gazette* cameraman. After that, we were to travel to the former Biederman home on Zeglarska Street. The producers had arranged for me to meet the family currently residing there. I hoped it wasn't the same guy that was there in 1945. Finally we would go to dinner at a new Jewish style restaurant called Anatevka. I thought to myself, Jewish style restaurant? I can't wait to see this. We then said goodnight and went to our rooms. When I finally jumped into bed I thought, all in all, it was a pretty good day. I survived almost a full day in Lodz.

I woke up the following morning, Monday the eleventh of October, at 8:00 a.m. and before breakfast went outside to check the weather. It was still frigid outside. We were scheduled to be picked up at 10:30 a.m. by Derek and then head to the Museum of Archaeology and Ethnography for our 11 a.m. meeting. I decided that after breakfast I would run over to the next-door shopping mall and buy a winter coat. The mall opened at 9:30, so I had time to shop and return to the hotel before Derek got there. I was waiting at the doors when the mall opened and after I went in, I found a store that had down parkas. I purchased one and then quickly made my way back to the hotel. I was now ready to face the frosty day.

At 10:30 I met the crew in the lobby and we waited for Derek. I got lots of compliments on my new black and orange, down filled winter coat. Derek soon arrived, and we all jumped in the van for the three-mile drive to the museum. The Museum of Archaeology and Ethnography was located in Plac Wolnscni, which is the central plaza of Lodz. In the center of the plaza there is a large obelisk. Mounted atop the obelisk is a statue of Polish war hero Tadeusz Kosciusko. Interestingly, there is also a statue of Tadeusz Kosciusko in downtown Detroit. He had volunteered his service to the fledgling American republic in their struggle against the British during the Revolutionary War; he later became an American General. Surrounding the plaza is the encircling terminus of Piotrkowska Street. The buildings of Plac Wolnosci are arranged in a circular pattern on the opposite side of the street from the obelisk. After doing the roundabout turn we stopped in front of the Museum of Archaeology and Ethnography. Although I had been inside of the museum on my previous trip to Lodz, at that time I was taken in through the rear service entrance, so this was my first time seeing the facade of the building. It was a large four-story yellow cement building with four cement columns at the front entrance. It looked kind of impressive. Hanging over the door was a blue plastic banner which read: "History of the Jews of Lodz" exhibition.

After the crew unloaded their equipment, we went inside where Joanna and a photographer from the *Lodz Gazette* were waiting. We met with one of the museum's directors and he explained that the Jewish exhibit was temporary and was done in conjunction with the events commemorating the sixtieth anniversary of the liberation of the Lodz Ghetto. Rohan decided it would be appropriate to film me touring the exhibit.

At the first station of the exhibit there was a very interesting map which ended up being a genealogic treasure trove for me. It was entitled "Jewish Immigration to Lodz." The map showed that at the turn of the nineteenth century there were only a handful of Jews in Lodz. As the cloth and textile industry began to grow in Lodz, the encouraging economic news and job opportunities attracted a lot of German and Jewish Immigrants from all over Europe. One of those places which Jews came from was the Netherlands.

In 1815, the Dutch economy collapsed due to the prolonged British naval blockade resulting from the Anglo-Dutch War of 1780. Many Dutch Jews left the Netherlands, especially from the hard-hit coastal Zeeland province and immigrated to Lodz. This information was a huge revelation for me, because I now likely knew why a large number of the coins in my family's collection were of Zeelandic origin. In my later research, I learned that each of the seven Dutch provinces minted its own coins until the unification of the Dutch mint in 1806. My family's coin collection contained coins from Zeelandia dating back to 1702. In fact, most of the coins in the family collection were from the Netherlands or one of those seven Dutch provinces prior to unification.

Just then, as I stood in front of the map, the realization hit me! For years, everyone I met would tell me that I don't look Jewish at all and in fact looked more like an Irishman. Remember, even Mishkel 2 himself mentioned that he thought I resembled an Irish soccer player. Being muscular and six foot three inches tall with reddish blond hair and blue eyes, I suddenly realized that I definitely ain't no Irishman; on the contrary, I'm a big Dutch Jew! Although Jews in the Diaspora mostly married amongst themselves, over their two thousand year history since the destruction of the second temple and their dispersion throughout Europe, some regional foreign DNA made its way into the Jewish gene pool. From the Jewish perspective, sometimes it happened willingly and other times not.

In the Central and Western European countries intermarriage between Jews and Gentiles was not all that uncommon. Of all the European countries, the Netherlands had among the highest intermarriage rates. This was not the case in Eastern Europe. In Poland, Ukraine, and Russia, for example, the intermarriage rate was virtually zero. Most of the non-Jewish

DNA was introduced during pogroms where violent raids including rape and pillage were common place. Of course, many of the rapes resulted in unplanned pregnancies. As a result, like it or not, the Jewish population began to assume a definitive local flavor.

As I continued to stare at the map of Jewish immigration to Lodz, I had another epiphany: As my ancestors moved from the Netherlands to Lodz they obviously brought the coins with them. It would not be a stretch to assume that many of them had been in my family's possession for over two hundred years.

After being overwhelmed by the revelations of the first map displayed in the Jewish history exhibit, we continued on through the museum. The remainder of the Jewish exhibit was mostly disappointing. There was one display case which contained tattered religious objects and the rest of the exhibit featured unflattering pictures taken in the poorer squalid Jewish neighborhoods of Lodz during the interwar years. There was very little information about the Holocaust and the fate of the Jewish community. When we finished the Jewish exhibit, there was one glaring omission; I didn't see the coins. Where were they? What happened to the Biederman family being synonymous with the Holocaust? Where was the display where generations would learn about the Holocaust with my father's family being one of the main examples of the destruction of the Jewish community? I asked the manager that was accompanying us where the coins were. He said that they were in another part of the museum and we were heading there next.

As we headed down a hallway we entered another room that had a sign over the entrance "Historical Coins of the World." As we entered the room we were guided to an all glass showcase situated in one corner. Inside the showcase, there they were, beautifully displayed on a purple velvet cloth in all their splendor: my family's coin collection. Each coin was exhibited standing on edge in a holder with a tag next to it detailing the year, denomination, and country of origin. Also included in the display case was the intact ceramic teapot. It was expertly reconstructed and if you didn't know, you would never be able to tell that it was once completely shattered. A sign on the wall over the coins gave the following description:

> Inside this showcase are the coins of the buried treasure found at 7 Zeglarska Street. The coins were discovered by Polish investigators acting on a tip from a descendent of a former resident of Lodz. After a thorough investigation and using ground penetrating radar technology, our researchers were able to locate these coins that were contained inside the displayed ceramic pot. The pot was shattered during the dig but reconstructed for this display.

The sign was of course in Polish and I was aided in reading it by Derek. I angrily told the manager using Derek as an interpreter: "So that's the way it's going to be, huh? Polish investigators? Some anonymous descendent of a Lodz resident? No mention of the Biedermans at all?" The manager didn't answer me. He ignored my questions and thanked us all for coming and wished the Canadian crew all the best and he hoped they would enjoy their time in Lodz. He then did an about face, quickly left the room, and disappeared. I stayed in the room and posed in front of the coins for some film and still pictures for the stunned *Past Lives* and *Lodz Gazette* crews.

We then left the museum. Once outside, Joanna asked if I would pose with the Canadian film crew in front of the museum. This picture would end up being on the cover of the next day's edition of the *Lodz Gazette*. Joanna then asked me what I thought of the feature article that she had written about my family which she sent me a few weeks ago. I responded that as of yet, I had not received it, but that wasn't all that surprising. I was on a Canada Post rural delivery route and foreign mail can take up to a month to reach me. She said she also enclosed a copy of the World War II history magazine that I interviewed for in Warsaw and other interesting

Lodz Gazette photo of me with the Canadian TV crew from *Past Lives*.

materials that I would enjoy. She wouldn't give me any more information than that, so as not to spoil the surprise when I opened the package. After my experience in the museum, I was already anxious to go home and wait for her letter. In spite of the improper placement of my coins and the snub I received at the museum, however, the visit was not a complete disappointment. I was actually appeased by the discovery of my Dutch genealogy. I just traced my roots back three hundred years and finally, I would be able to tell people why I was Aryan looking, and did not look like a nice Jewish boy.

Joanna and the cameraman from the *Lodz Gazette* had to leave to cover another story after taking the photos of me and the *Past Lives* crew in front of the museum. Karen, the *Past Lives* production coordinator, told us we had a couple of hours until we were scheduled to meet the family at 7 Zeglarska Street. Since we were at 14 Plac Wolnosci, which was the address of the museum, I told the crew the story of my father's childhood photos and how I later discovered the stamp on the back with the address of the photographer at 2 Plac Wolnosci. We decided to walk the short distance to see if the studio was still there.

To my surprise, a photography studio was still in operation at that location. We went inside and talked to the owners. They were a husband and wife team and both were photographers. They told us they had recently purchased the studio from the previous longtime owner after he decided to retire. I told them that my father was here in the 1920s with his family and showed them one of the pictures I brought with me. The husband then showed us around the studio. It was a two-story building with a reception desk and a couple of small offices on the first floor. The second floor contained the studio complete with an elaborate lighting system and a large set of scenic backdrops which were on reels which could be electronically raised or lowered. He said he just replaced the old backdrops with these new modern ones. He then took us to a storage room and took out some old backdrops on a wooden reel. The photographer was excited when he was able to find the exact backdrop that was used for the picture of my father and his sisters. He then hung it in the studio and I had my picture taken in front of it. We also did a film shoot of this for the *Past Lives* show. It was very eerie for me as I realized that I was likely standing in the exact spot that my father had stood all those years ago. I imagined his proud parents in the background fawning over their little boy as he was having professional photographs taken. Little did they know what terrible fate awaited them in just a few short years. It was difficult for me to maintain my composure and not break down and sob while I was having my picture taken.

After taking my picture, the Polish photographer replaced the old worn backdrop. He then showed us another storage closet. Inside this closet there were numerous boxes full of photo negatives on glass slides. He said the previous owner told him these negatives were there when he bought the place. This most recent owner told me that my father's portraits were probably contained on those slides since they were from the 1920s and 1930s. Unfortunately, the thousands of glass negatives were all thrown in boxes in no particular order. He said I was welcome to look through them. Regrettably, I responded that there were way too many for me to look through in the short time I was scheduled to be in Lodz. I again became very emotional when I realized that my father and his sisters' images were laying somewhere forgotten here in this heap. In a disturbing way, these negatives were kind of a metaphor of the Holocaust.

After our visit to the photo studio, the next stop on our agenda was my father's childhood home at 7 Zeglarska Street. I don't know how the *Past Lives* producers got a hold of the family that lived there, and I was quite surprised that they agreed to meet with me. I figured this can't be the same resident that was there in 1945 because there is no way that that person would want to see me. Unless, he possibly thought I didn't know about the shooting of my father's friend; or maybe my mother had the story all wrong. I didn't really know what to think at this point. Either way, now that the coins were found, I really didn't have any interest in going back to the home. I knew, however, that it was critical to the story that the house be featured, so I agreed to a visit.

As we drove north up Zgierska Street, I was getting more nervous as we got closer to our left turn onto Zeglarska Street. When we reached the home, there was a couple about my age (late thirties or early forties) waiting for us in the walkway. I didn't know what to say to them and I didn't know what they knew, so I thought I would just keep quiet. The homeowners happily showed the *Past Lives* crew around the yard and then took them to the site where the coins were found. They seemed very friendly and appeared to be enjoying their time on Canadian TV. I was content to stay in the background, but then the attention turned to me as the Polish homeowners walked over and using Derek as an interpreter said: "You must be the son of the guy who buried the coins here." He reached out his hand; I shook it and kept my answer short and sweet: "Yes I am." The moment was very awkward for me because I didn't know if this guy was play acting or was just a nice guy genuinely unaware that there was a potential shooting here. I was recalling my mother's story about my father's friend being shot in 1945 during their initial attempt to retrieve the coins. He then asked if we would like to come in and see the home. Before I could decline, Rohan said that would be great. For my part, with my discomfort level reaching a boiling point, I would have rather just gotten the hell out of there. When we went inside the home, there was an old man, likely in his eighties, sitting stone faced at the kitchen table. The husband introduced him as his grandfather and then kept moving through the house. The man just sat there motionless and expressionless as Derek introduced us. I was puzzled by this old man. Was he just a typical older Pole, untrusting of Jews and foreigners? Or maybe he was actually a nice guy but the language barrier prevented him from socializing with us. Maybe he was just senile and didn't know who we were and what was going on. The fourth possibility was the most frightening. Was this the man that shot my father's friend in 1945?

The situation was very difficult for me. I was tempted to ask Derek to ask the old man if he lived here in 1945 when my father had attempted to retrieve the coins. If he said no, then I would be wondering if he was telling the truth. Could I actually expect him to say that yes he was the man who was living here and was also the one who killed my father's friend? If on the other hand he said yes, then the situation becomes even more difficult. Do I follow up with the question: did you shoot somebody at that time? What if he said yes he did? What happens then? I was getting deeply disturbed. I decided to just shut up and dragged myself through the house for the tour. Fortunately it was a very small house and we were out in minutes. Derek then thanked the grandson and wished him well. The grandson asked Derek to ask me if I had any questions. If only this guy knew the questions I had! Then again, maybe his grandfather was the shooter and he knew it all along. Is this what he was trying to get me to ask? How do I approach the situation? If these guys knew what happened in 1945, their information would be priceless for me. On the other hand, it could also be extremely dangerous. Would they be comfortable with me knowing what happened there? I ended up telling the grandson that I didn't have any questions and was more than grateful for the time he already spent with us. I just really needed to get out of there. I was grateful when the grandson said, "Well then, it was nice meeting you," shook everybody's hand and went back in the house. I breathed a huge sigh of relief when we got in Derek's van and when the van door slid shut and we were on our way. I must say that the couple living in the house were very pleasant during the visit and had I not heard my mother's story, I would have been much more at ease. I probably would have thought they were the nicest Polish people I have ever met. As we drove away from 7 Zeglarska Street, I hoped that either this was not the family that was here in 1945 or that my mother's story was not true. Since I didn't know, I would have to include this question in my growing list of unanswered and unanswerable questions I had about my father's history.

As we drove back towards downtown Lodz, Karen the production coordinator noticed the anti-Semitic graffiti that was ubiquitous in the Baluty section. She asked Derek what's up with that. He gave an absurd explanation which I guess has become the official Lodz party line. After I was there on this trip in 2004, I have heard from many people who have been on Jewish Heritage tours to Lodz since then that have been offered the same explanation for the graffiti. According to Derek, the graffiti wasn't anti-Semitic at all. He explained that soccer is very popular in Lodz and that there are a couple of teams who have very passionate fans. These two teams and their fan bases have a very intense rivalry. The graffiti, he explained, is written by the fans of one team calling the other team "Jews" and then hanging them. "Jews" in this case, does not mean Jews in the traditional sense. "Jew" or the Star of David has just become an insulting swear word or symbol in the modern colloquial Polish vernacular. It's kind of like "son of a bitch" he said. So when one paints the Star of David next to a team or person's name, he is just calling them a "son of a bitch," but that doesn't mean he wishes any ill will on those people of the Jewish religion. "Well then, that's wonderful, so the name and national emblem of my people has become a Polish swear word. Now that we've cleared that up, I feel much better," I said. I then asked, "What about all the Holocaust monuments located all over Poland that I have seen which have been defaced with that same Star of David on the hangman's noose?"

"Ah, those are anti-Semites and not soccer fans who did that," answered Derek.

As we were finishing our discussion on the difference between anti-Semitic and non-anti-Semitic graffiti from the Polish logical point of view, we arrived at our next stop. It was the "Jewish style" restaurant that Karen had mentioned the previous night. It seemed to me that someone in the Lodz Chamber of Commerce finally realized what Warsaw and Krakow businessmen realized a few years earlier: Jewish tourism can be a tremendous source of revenue. There are many descendants of the 300,000 Polish-Jewish Holocaust survivors anxious to see their parents' or grandparents' home towns. In that case, as painful as it may be, it's not a bad idea to make your city as Jewish friendly as is possible. Events like the nearly yearlong sixtieth anniversary commemoration of the liquidation of the Lodz Ghetto were a good start. Opening Jewish friendly shops and especially restaurants was an even better one. This restaurant was an attempt at that ideal.

The restaurant was called Anatevka, it was named after the fictional town in the Ukraine from the classic play and later movie: *Fiddler on the Roof.* The font on the sign on the front of the restaurant was made to look like Hebrew letters. So far, so good, I thought. Then, we walked in. There in the lobby was a bearded mannequin dressed like a Hassidic Jew, complete with a tallis (shawl worn by Jews while praying in a synagogue) wrapped around its shoulders. The mannequin had a stereotypical large nose and purplish skin. It looked like a caricature right out of the Nazi era, virulently anti-Semitic newspaper *Der Sturmer*, whose publisher, by the way, Julius Streicher, was convicted of crimes against humanity and was executed at Nuremberg in 1946. To add insult to injury, the mannequin was hunched over an antique cash register full of imitation gold coins. While the non-Jewish crew thought this thing was harmless and cute, I was completely disgusted and couldn't believe the overt anti-Semitic reference. Especially now that I was here in Lodz filming a television show about gold coins. I wondered if my story was the inspiration for this repulsive mannequin. Despite my revulsion to the mannequin, I agreed to go in and eat. When we entered the dining room there was a girl sitting on a perch near the ceiling playing Jewish music on her violin. Her repertoire included the entire score from *Fiddler on the Roof.* She was actually quite good, and the music began to soothe the savage beast that had arisen in me after seeing the ridiculous display in the lobby.

As I sat peering at the menu, I actually started to enjoy sitting in this restaurant. Listening to the Jewish music reminded me of my childhood growing up in a Jewish home in Detroit. We had one of those big cabinet stereo systems that were popular in the 1960s in our family room. On the weekends my father would often listen to music. I believe he only had two records: The original soundtrack to *Fiddler on the Roof* and the best of the Barry Sisters. The Barry sisters were two Jewish Bronx born singers who were very popular with Jewish listeners in the 1950s and 1960s.

Picture from Anatevka Restaurant.

Their real name was Bagelman, little wonder why they found it necessary to change it, and they were the daughters of a Russian immigrant father and Hungarian mother. All of their songs were sung in Yiddish. I would have really felt at home if during the violinist's breaks, the restaurant would have played the Barry sisters through the stereo system instead of the scratched old Polish records that were playing. As my anger over the lobby abomination subsided, I figured I would give this place a pass and chalk it up to ignorance instead of anti-Semitism. Today, there are virtually no Jews remaining in Lodz, so maybe this restauranteur had never seen one and actually thought that the mannequin was what real Jews looked like. The coin reference was a little harder to overlook.

As I opened the menu and began to read, it was actually filled with Jewish sounding items. I ordered the gefilte fish appetizer and the cholent (traditional Jewish Eastern European stew) dinner. My mother was a terrible cook and only made two things well: cholent and gefilte fish. Consequently, my diet featured a steady portion of these two items. This restaurant was becoming a real stroll down memory lane for me; and then the food arrived.

There are two things for certain that I have learned in my life. One is that you can put perfume on a pig, but in the end, it's still a pig. The second is that you can call Polish prepared food by a Jewish name, but in the end it's still Polish prepared food. This stuff that I ate tasted nothing like what I grew up eating in my mother's kitchen or in any other Jewish household or catered Jewish event, for that matter. It was in fact, quite awful. Thankfully the *Past Lives* crew ordered a couple bottles of Polish vodka and with them I was able to wash this dreck down. The Polish vodka was extremely potent. My mother used to give me a few drops of Polish vodka mixed with water to gargle with when I had a sore throat as a kid. The vodka was the only positive thing about the entire meal.

After we finished eating, the waitress brought the check and I couldn't believe what came with it. As a memento of our visit, each guest received a mini clay figurine of a rabbi clutching an authentic Polish uncirculated penny. Each of the three different styles of figurines was molded in such a way that a penny could be snapped in place under one or both arms, depending on the model. I couldn't believe what I was seeing; it was surreal. I was stunned that this place could remain in business. The food was awful, and they went out of their way to insult the very clientele that they were attempting to attract. I guessed that there was enough new Jewish tourism flowing into Lodz to keep this place afloat; the repeat business must be non-existent. As I write this book in June 2017, Anatevka is still in operation! The ghastly mannequin is still in the lobby and they are still handing out the rabbinical clay figurines clutching the Polish penny.

Upon further evaluation, I concluded that places like this restaurant serve a purpose and are the reason why all the Jewish Heritage Tours begin in Poland and finish in Israel. Lodz and its environs are a veritable theme park of anti-Semitism. Experience Poland (especially Lodz) and then continue on to Israel to be uplifted and understand the importance of the Jewish State.

For my part, I was relieved that this would be my last night in Lodz. Before departing the restaurant, Karen gave us our next day's itinerary. We were invited to meet with the Deputy Mayor and City Council for breakfast at the Lodz city hall at 9:30 the following morning. It was my understanding that the Mayor was out on medical leave. I was not sure whether or not this medical leave was related to the incident in April when the Mayor collapsed at 7 Zeglarska Street during the coin dig. After the city hall meeting, we were to film a final scene in Lodz in front of the Moses statue in the Main Park and then mercifully depart for the three hour drive to Wroclaw. We left the restaurant and piled into Derek's van for the ride back to the Ibis hotel.

When I got to my room, before going to bed, as I replayed the events of the day, Alexander Solzhenitsyn's classic novel *One Day in the Life of Ivan Denisovich* came to mind. It was the story of Ivan's single day in the Russian gulag. As I slipped under the covers, I felt a greater empathy for the main character and then thought, after my day in Lodz, Ivan has nothing on me!

After I awoke in the morning of Tuesday, October the 12, I quickly went down to the hotel lobby to purchase the daily edition of the *Lodz Gazette*. I found myself pictured on the front cover standing in front of the Museum of Ethnography and Archaeology with the *Past Lives* television crew. At first, I was grateful that there weren't any pictures of me with the coin collection. I didn't want the owners of Anatevka to be able to say "See, we told you so, we were right about these Jews all along." But then I got to thinking: Who are these people kidding? The Poles are the ones desperately clinging to the coins. If the owners of Anatevka really wanted to portray the situation accurately, they would have figurines resembling the Mayor, the museum curator, and the Minister of Culture clutching the coins. Those should be the three caricatures on the model figurines that they're handing out. For my part, I realized I didn't give a damn about the value of these coins; this quest was a process of healing for me. My father died in 1981, but I had kept his memory very much alive and with me for the past twenty years. What these Poles thought, suddenly meant nothing to me. Who are they to judge me, and why should I care what they think? As I began to feel reinvigorated, I grabbed a coffee and waited for the crew and Derek to meet me in the lobby at 9:00 a.m. for the trip to city hall.

It was only a short drive up Piotrkowska Street to the city hall. When we arrived, the crew unloaded their equipment and began filming. Almost on cue, a woman about my age ran out of the office and hugged me and then kissed both of my cheeks. She then introduced herself as the Deputy Mayor. She continued: "Welcome home, we're so happy to have a native son of Lodz back home. Lodz is so proud of you and we're so proud of our Jewish heritage. Jews have contributed so much to the city. We are so happy with the Jewish revival currently happening in the Lodz." I felt like I was part of a television commercial being filmed for Canadian Jewish audiences promoting Lodz tourism. Jewish revival? Where? Granted there was a new statue, in front of the city hall on Piotrkowska Street, of Lodz born Jewish pianist Arthur Rubinstein, but that doesn't a Jewish Revival make. The Deputy Mayor then invited us in for breakfast and said she was eager to learn all about my history. We were escorted into the city council conference room where breakfast was set up on a large oak conference table. Set around the table were about twenty modern high-backed leather chairs. I was very impressed with the modern appearance and amenities of this room. The Deputy Mayor invited us to sit down and then introduced each member of the City Council that was present. Set out on silver serving platters in front of us were lox, bagels, and cream cheese. Although it is a little stereotypical, you can never go wrong with offering a Jewish lox, bagels, and cream cheese. There was also a tea and coffee set on the table. I made myself at home with a couple of bagels and a coffee and then began to tell my story to the Lodz City Officials. I told them how my father died many years ago and how I went on this quest to learn about the story of his life that I never knew. I said that only after his death did I learn the fact that he was from Lodz and was one of four children and the only boy. I then told them about Eichmann's order and my theory of when the coins were buried. I continued with the fate of his entire family and how my father survived the war. They were most impressed with the fact that he was on Schindler's List.

I have always been amazed by the response elicited whenever I have mentioned Schindler's List. Whenever I say the words "Schindler's List," I notice the sudden raised eyebrows of even the most previously disinterested listener. It is a testament to the power and lasting influence of that movie.

I then completed my story without mentioning the possible postwar shooting incident involving my father and his friend. After I was finished, the council members sat in stunned silence for a moment as if this was their first time hearing the retelling of the tragic events of the World War II.

The Deputy Mayor then got up and thanked me and the television crew for coming and wished us the best. With that she handed me an envelope and said, "I know it has taken a while, but this is for you." I opened the envelope and removed the small slip of paper that was contained inside. It was a newly issued birth certificate, complete with the official stamp of the City of Lodz, for Hersz (the Polish spelling) Biederman born September 7, 1925. I knew it! I was right! The Poles have had these records all along! It took me a while to regain my composure, but after I had, I asked the Deputy Mayor if the birth certificates for my father's sisters were also available. She responded that Joanna Podolska had already requested and received the birth certificates for the three Biederman sisters. I was shocked. I couldn't believe it was finally true. I was finally going to learn the names and birthdays of my long-lost aunts. With this discovery, I will have finally made good on my vow of that day in 1984 when I first stumbled on three old, long forgotten black and white photos tucked away in my father's nightstand.

As I sat in the council chambers contemplating what just happened, my moment of deep introspection was interrupted by one of the city council members. He offered to shake my hand and then said it was unfortunate that the Ministry had decided to keep the coins. He then told me that now that I was in possession of my father's birth certificate, in accordance with the circumstances of war and international law, I was eligible to apply for Polish citizenship. I thanked him for the information and tried to keep a straight face. What the hell am I going to do with Polish Citizenship? Wait a minute, I thought to myself, maybe I could try out for the Polish Olympic Hockey team. I could take my mother's murdered brother Henryk's spot. If only I were twenty years younger!

After wrapping up at the city hall we departed for our final stop in Lodz: the Moses statue, officially known as the *Decalogue*, situated in Staromiejski Park. The park was located just north of Plac Wolnosci and was a short drive up Piotrkowska Street from the city hall. Staromiejski literally means old town and the park was built on the site that had been the old town market square. The square once was a bustling center of daily life in prewar Jewish Lodz and the ornate "Altschul" or old synagogue once stood there. The "Altschul" was built in 1861 and remodeled over a three-year period from 1897 to 1900. The Lodzers whom I have spoken to said it was the most beautiful synagogue in all of Europe. The synagogue was set on fire and destroyed by the Germans on November 15, 1939. Also destroyed in the fire were the thirty-six Torah scrolls that it contained. The Moses statue was erected in 1995 on the approximate site where the Altschul once stood as a memorial to the destroyed Jewish community of Lodz. Today it stands over a now vacant cobblestone square. Surrounding the square are the tree lined grounds of Staromiejski Park. For me, the place felt eerily similar to Jedwabne.

RZECZPOSPOLITA POLSKA

Województwo .... łódzkie ....

Urząd Stanu Cywilnego w ...... Łódź – Centrum ....

ODPIS SKRÓCONY AKTU URODZENIA

1. Nazwisko .... Biderman ─────────────

2. Imię (imiona) .... Hersz Mendel ─────────────

3. Data urodzenia .. siódmego września tysiąc dziewięćset dwudzie-

.. stego piątego (07.09.1925) roku ─────────────

4. Miejsce urodzenia .... Łódź ─────────────

5. Imię (imiona) i nazwisko rodowe .... Lipa Biderman ─────────
(ojca)

6. Imię (imiona) i nazwisko rodowe .... Estera Małka Lewkowicz ──────
(matki)

Poświadcza się zgodność powyższego odpisu

z treścią aktu urodzenia Nr IV.1123(45)26

Łódź ,dnia 09.07.2001r

KIEROWNIK
Urzędu Stanu Cywilnego

M-8 WA Łódź, tel 632-55-31

My father's birth certificate.

For the *Past Lives* film shoot, I stood under the Moses monument as I gave my impressions of what we had experienced the last few days in Lodz. The monument was about thirty feet tall and consisted of a dark gray sculpture of Moses carrying the stone tablets engraved with the Ten Commandments on his back. The statue was mounted on a brown marble pedestal. I thought it was a dark, depressing piece of art and was apropos for Lodz. While I reminisced for the film shoot about the cemetery, the museum, the photo studio, and the house on Zeglarska Street, I noticed an old man, probably in his eighties, intensely watching the proceedings while lurking in the background. I completed the film segment by telling the film director that the most lasting and disappointing impression of Lodz, from my point of view, was the complete exclusion or of any mention of my father or his family at the coin exhibit in the Museum of Ethnography and Archaeology.

After we finished the film shoot and while the crew was packing up their equipment, the aforementioned old man walked up and introduced himself. He spoke perfect, albeit German accented English. He started off by telling me that he had been following my story for the past six months and was glad he was able to find me. He went on to tell me that he was a municipal police officer in Lodz before the war and was recruited to join the SS in 1939, after the Germans occupied the city. He was sworn in as a member of the SS Ordnungspolizei in November of 1939. One of his first duties, he said, was to help with the initial round up of Jews that were to be deported to Krosno. He said he was now a born again Christian and he regretted what he did during the war.

I was stunned. I didn't know how to react. During my teenage years I often thought about what I would do if I ever found an SS man alive, even though I never expected or believed that it could happen. Suddenly, here I was, face to face with one. Before I could react, he went on to ask me if Jews of my generation could ever find forgiveness for the German and Polish nations. I told him that Jews of my generation didn't have the authority to forgive. Forgiveness, I told him, would have to come from my father or his sisters or his parents; but unfortunately, they are no longer with us, so I told him: "I guess you're out of luck"; I then turned and walked away back towards the film crew. The old man followed right behind me. As I stopped and turned around, just before I was ready to tell him to get lost or possibly deck him, he reached into his jacket pocket and pulled out a page from the *Lodz Gazette* dated May 7, 2004. The page was from Joanna Podolska's feature story about the coins and included the pictures of my father and his sisters that I gave her to photocopy back in April. I took the page of newspaper from the old Nazi to look at the article more closely, since I had never seen it before. I was still waiting for my copy that Joanna had sent me. I imagined it was somewhere in a mail bin in some office of the Canadian Postal Service. The SS man said that he keeps the article with him and he thinks of my father's family whenever he goes to pray. He then reached out his hand and looked at me with a look of desperation hoping that I would shake it. I hesitated for a moment and then reached out and shook his hand. I immediately regretted it; I couldn't believe I just shook this Nazi's hand! The SS man, conversely, suddenly straightened up and smiled, he had a look of tremendous relief. He looked like a man who just had a terrible burden lifted off his shoulders; one that he had been carrying around with him for sixty-five years. He said *dzienkuje* ("thank you" in Polish) and quickly turned and walked out of the square and disappeared into Staromiejski Park. He left without taking back the page of newspaper. I don't know if he forgot it or if he thought he no longer needed it. Either way, I tucked it into my jacket. I still have it to this day.

As I stood in the square gathering my thoughts, I suddenly felt a surge of energy through my body. I felt like the emperor who just pardoned some worthless man of a serious crime. I didn't feel ashamed to be the son of Holocaust survivors anymore. For years, the stigma of the Jews going like sheep to the slaughter was a badge of shame I carried inside of me. Now I realized the shame was on them, the guys like the SS man who just left. My father and mother were kids when these guys came with guns. Yet they faced it all: Mengele, Hitler, Auschwitz; my mother even snatched her mother from certain death at the gate to the gas chamber, and they stood tall and survived. Now, as this SS man was groveling in front of me, I felt a sense of relief and pride. I realized that with that handshake, both of our burdens were removed that day. Despite the freezing cold, I unzipped my new down jacket and unbuttoned the top buttons of my shirt; I didn't feel the need to hide my Star of David from these people anymore. With that, I walked back to Derek's van where the film crew was loading their equipment. "Who was that man?" Karen asked. "Oh, no one," I responded, "just a guy looking for directions."

After we all got back in the van for the drive back to the Ibis hotel, I removed my father's birth certificate to take a closer look. I was disappointed when I noticed that unlike mine, issued by the State of Michigan, my father's birth certificate did not contain an address of residence for the birth parents. I was disappointed that I still had no documentation to prove that he ever lived at 7 Zeglarska Street. We made a quick stop at the hotel to grab our bags and check out, and then it was off to Wroclaw for the next stop on our journey. It had been quite an emotional rollercoaster ride through that once bustling, heavily Jewish textile manufacturing town, which was now a blighted and Jew free urban zone known as Lodz.

Wroclaw

Our last film location was scheduled to be the Gross-Rosen Concentration Camp in Rogoznica, Poland. The *Past Lives* production staff thought Gross-Rosen was an important piece of the story and wanted a lot of footage from there. As mentioned earlier, they thought that any story in which the events of Holocaust were an important element, needed to show a concentration camp. They decided that in order to allow plenty of time for filming, it would best for the crew to be there when it opened at 8:00 in the morning of Wednesday, October 13. That day was also scheduled to be our last full day in Poland. In order to avoid making the four-hour drive from Lodz on that Wednesday morning, it was decided we should stay in Wroclaw on Tuesday night, which was the nearest major city. Wroclaw was only about thirty-five miles, which was a one hour drive on Polish rural roads, from Rogoznica, and also had an airport that we could depart from on our return trip home. Rogoznica was in the southwestern corner of Poland near the Czech border and was close to Brunnlitz, Oscar Schindler's hometown. I was looking forward to seeing Wroclaw and Gross-Rosen for myself and also didn't mind saying goodbye to Lodz.

It was a three-hour drive from Lodz to Wroclaw. Wroclaw was actually a German city before the war and was named Breslau. Breslau was the last major German city to surrender during World War II. On August 24, 1944 with the Red Army about to enter Poland, Hitler declared Breslau a fortress city. It was to be defended to the last man and never surrendered. He thought possession of Breslau was of great strategic importance in disrupting the Soviets March on Berlin.

As the Red Army advanced on Breslau, Karl Hanke, the German Gauleiter of the Silesian region was named city battle commander by Hitler. He ordered the civilian population to be evacuated on January 19, 1945 in preparation for the upcoming Soviet assault. Due to heavy Soviet shelling almost all modes of transportation out of the city were disabled. Many left Breslau on foot and died in the freezing temperatures. Those civilians who opted to stay in the city were soon trapped. The city was besieged on February 13 as part of the lower Silesian offensive operation by troops of the 1st Ukrainian front of the Red Army. It was completely encircled two days later. After the airport was lost to the Soviets, the Germans built a makeshift runway in the middle of the city, destroying many buildings in the process, so that the encircled garrison could be supplied by air. The besieged German garrison held out until May 6, two days before the war ended and six days after Hitler committed suicide.

During the fighting 70 percent of the buildings in Breslau were destroyed including most of the ornate "old town" with its renowned thirteenth-century gothic architecture. One group of buildings that weren't destroyed in the fighting were the many synagogues in Breslau. They had already been destroyed by the German inhabitants seven years earlier, on Kristallnacht in November 1938. It is also estimated between 80,000 and 150,000 German civilians died in the fighting.

Prior to the anticipated end of World War II, the leaders of the Allied nations, Josef Stalin from the Soviet Union, Winston Churchill of the United Kingdom, and Franklin Delano Roosevelt of the United States, collectively known as the Big Three, met at Yalta in the Crimea during February 1945 to determine how Europe would be carved up after the war. Under the terms agreed on at the Yalta Conference, after the war was over, Poland's prewar borders were shifted westward. The city of Breslau was transferred to Poland and became Wroclaw. Soon Poles began arriving from the eastern areas like Lvov, which were now part of the Soviet Union. In order to make room for them, most of the ethnic German population was expelled back into what remained of Germany. A massive building campaign was then undertaken by the Polish government to restore Wroclaw to its former grandeur. It was mostly completed by 1962. I was eager to see the results.

As we entered the outskirts of Wroclaw after our three-hour drive from Lodz, the first structure I saw was a huge circular eighty-foot-high concrete bunker and air raid shelter built by the Nazis in 1942. It had four-foot-thick exterior concrete walls. From the looks of this massive structure, it was obvious to me that the Germans were planning on turning the city into a fortress even at that early juncture of the war. From the bunker it was only a short drive to our hotel which was located on an Islet in the middle of the Oder River. The Oder River rises in the Czech Republic and flows through western Poland before turning north and emptying into the Baltic Sea. The northern part of the Oder forms the northern border between Poland and Germany after it intersects with the Neisse River which forms the southern portion. The City of Wroclaw is bisected by the southern portion of the Oder River.

As we drove to our hotel called the Hotel Tumski, named after the Tumski Islet on which it was located, I was quite taken with the beauty of the city. There are many islets in the Oder and therefore numerous bridges throughout the city. There were many ornate Gothic buildings, each of different shape and color. When we checked into the hotel, I was surprised to hear the front office staff speaking German. I guessed there was still a significant ethnic German population living in the city. The rooms in the hotel were very small and basic, which was typical of Soviet era lodgings.

After we dropped our belongings into our rooms we took the short walk across a bridge to the Old Town Market square on the south side of the Oder to explore the city and find a place to eat dinner. According to one of the brochures in the hotel, the market square (called a *rynek* in Polish) in Wroclaw is the largest one in all of Europe. It had many shops, restaurants, and outdoor cafes. Each adjoining building featured its own unique color and architecture. Most of buildings' facades featured the arches with high towers and spires of various shapes and sizes that are typical of Gothic architecture. Each building also had its own unique lace stone wall carvings and window tracings. There were also stone statues and sculptures carved into the various supporting columns and buttresses. It was very breathtaking and something I hadn't seen the likes of anywhere in Poland. Overall, I was very impressed with the reconstruction job done in this city. For me, the place was a much needed one-night respite from the depressing history that we were previously exploring for the past few days. We ate dinner at a cafe in the market square and then headed back to the hotel. Karen reminded us to be up early for the trip to Gross-Rosen in the morning. It was back to the serious business for me.

Gross-Rosen

We departed Wroclaw at seven in the morning and arrived at Gross-Rosen shorty before it opened at 8:00 a.m. We stopped in at the former SS mess and recreation hall which was now the state museum, archive and administration building. It was located just outside of the main entrance gate and guardhouse. Waiting to give us a tour of the camp was a very attractive Polish woman in her late twenties or early thirties who was an archivist at the museum. I was tempted to ask the age-old trite question: "What's a girl like you doing in a place like this?" I resisted, however. It was another frigid October day, with the temperature hovering near the freezing mark. The date was October 13, 2004 which was two days short of being exactly sixty years from the day my father first arrived here on October 15, 1944.

Gross-Rosen was opened in 1940 and was originally a small slave labor camp for political prisoners forced to work in the adjacent SS owned stone quarry. In 1942, after the idea of using

Drawing that my father made which I believe depicts the Schindler Jews being marched into Gross-Rosen Concentration Camp. I found this in his nightstand three years after his death.

Jewish slave laborers as factory workers became official Nazi policy, it was greatly expanded and became a concentration camp for primarily Jewish prisoners forced to work in the German armaments factories constructed on the camp grounds or nearby. Some of the German companies which set up factories in Gross-Rosen and benefited from the Jewish slave labor were Daimler-Benz, IG Farben, Siemens, and Krupp. Gross-Rosen was not an extermination camp; its inmates died here as a result of disease, starvation or were worked to death. They toiled under atrocious conditions with insufficient food, sanitation and housing. In addition to working extremely long hours, Gross-Rosen workers were routinely whipped and beaten by the SS guards, who were reputed to be among the cruelest in the entire camp system. Mortality rate in the camp was around 33 percent.

My father never mentioned anything to me about Gross-Rosen, but after reading the memoirs of some of the Schindler's List survivors and speaking with a few others, I was able to accurately piece together the story of his experience there.

My father arrived, along with the seven hundred other male Schindler Jews, at the Gross-Rosen train station on Sunday October 15, 1944 after a six-hour train ride from Krakow/Plaszow. It was nighttime, and a steady freezing rain was falling. The loudspeaker at the station ordered him and his fellow prisoners to disembark at once. Waiting on the platform to receive them were the SS men dressed in their winter trench coats with their snarling Alsatian Shepherds restrained by a leash in one hand and a riding whip in the other. As soon as the Jews were all out of the train they were ordered to march out of the station and were

Another of my father's drawings.

prompted by a few cracks in the back with the SS men's whips. The Jews were wearing nothing more than their striped prison wool pants and shirts and worn out leather boots. After marching through the town of Gross-Rosen, all the while hurried along with the constant blows from the SS men's whips, they arrived, soaking wet, at the main entrance into the camp thirty minutes later. Underneath the big granite arch of the guardhouse that was inscribed with the words "Arbeit macht frei" the gates were opened, and the Jews were led to the *appelplatz* (assembly square) situated just inside. From there they were ordered to strip naked and wait for further instructions. As my father and his fellow prisoners stood naked in the mud, the ice-cold rain continued to fall. His clothes were soon collected by prison workers and taken away to be fumigated.

At the time of the Schindler Jews arrival, the German administration of Gross-Rosen was desperately trying to control the raging typhus epidemic that was ravaging the entire labor camp system. Before any new arriving prisoners would be allowed into the barracks, they were first subject to disinfection. Their clothes were removed and fumigated, and each prisoner was sprayed with the insecticide DDT in order to kill the lice which carried the typhus causing bacteria. When my father's group arrived, they had to wait outside in the rain and freezing temperatures for the disinfecting crew to come and set up the disinfecting station inside one of the barracks. This took several hours. Finally at dawn they were taken into the disinfection room and, after each man went through the process, they were then sent to another barrack to wait for their uniforms.

The new barrack was very small and had a bare wood floor and no furniture. The men were ordered to sit with their legs apart to allow the next man to squeeze in. They sat jammed in this position for many hours, until finally they were ordered to the next barrack to collect their uniforms, always being coaxed along by the end of the SS men's whips. As the whipping continued, the Jews grabbed whatever shirt and pants and shoes they could find before being hurried along to the next barrack. As they were dressing in their new barracks, my father was able to trade one of the two left shoes he received for a right one. The Schindler Jews were then ordered to assemble outside for roll call. After that was completed they were given a bowl of watery soup. It was their first meal since boarding the train in Plaszow twenty-four hours earlier.

The Schindler Jews were kept separate from the rest of the camp population during the one week they were at Gross-Rosen. On October 23, they were again marched to the train station by the SS while being heavily beaten. Finally they were loaded onto a train and taken to the safe haven of Oscar Schindler's new factory in Brunnlitz, Czechoslovakia. Many of the survivors I have talked to said that the week in Gross-Rosen was the most difficult thing that they have ever had to endure. Many continued to suffer from long term health consequences as a result of their stay.

One of the things I remember about my father was how much he hated the cold weather. Often his right foot would swell and he would suffer alternating numbness followed by severe pain upon warming. He told me that it was a consequence of frost injury he contracted "in the camps." He said he had contracted gangrene in his right foot, and the camp doctors were going to amputate it. After much pleading he said they agreed to surgically remove the dead tissue and attempt to treat the injury. Miraculously after one month he recovered and was able to keep his foot. Only after many years of research after his death, did I realize that my father's injury occurred as a direct result of that October night in Gross-Rosen. Fortunately for him, he was somehow able to limp to the Gross-Rosen train station and make it to Schindler's factory where he was able to receive proper medical care.

It is a testament to his fortitude and toughness that he was able to make the nearly three-kilometer walk to the train station on a rotting foot without a detectable limp. Any limping or crippled Jew would have been immediately shot by the SS. Any Jew unable to keep up would have been pounced on by the unleashed Alsatian Shepherds, as the SS guards watched in amusement.

We started our tour of Gross-Rosen from the administration building and walked towards the main camp gate. So far, our group was the first and only visitors in the camp that day. The entrance gate consisted of a guardhouse built atop a large granite archway. Inscribed on the archway in affixed black letters was the sarcastic Nazi phrase: "Arbeit macht frei." Inside the archway were two swinging metal gates. On either side of the arch were wooden guard barracks. Before reaching the gate, we passed the ruins of the SS kennels. Before I saw these kennels, I often wondered why prisoners didn't try to escape as they were being led out of the gate to the various factories. Once I realized that as they walked to these factories they were followed by a couple dozen trained, vicious, Alsatian attack dogs, I had my answer.

After we entered the gate we immediately came upon the *appelplatz* where my father stood naked in the freezing rain sixty years earlier. It was almost hard to believe that I was standing on the very same spot. I wondered if in my father's wildest dreams he could have ever envisioned that one day his son would be back to visit. At the far end of the square was a gallows where prisoners were forced to watch the public executions of other prisoners who broke the camp rules or tried to escape. We walked past the *appelplatz* to a path that led to the massive granite quarry. The quarry was full of rusting machinery and was now abandoned and flooded. When we returned to the camp we walked to the execution wall where prisoners were shot for a variety of offenses. Today it is covered with memorial plaques. Most of the buildings and barracks that made up Gross-Rosen are no longer standing. There was one rebuilt barrack set up to give the visitor an idea of what they looked like when the camp was operating. The barrack was a block cement building with three tiers of wooden bunks inside. After viewing the barrack, we finished the tour of the camp grounds by walking past the Siemens workshops and a large steel crematorium with a thirty-foot-high chimney. There was one watchtower left standing as well as much of the barbed wire fencing.

After we walked out through the main camp gate, we then toured the museum that was located in the administration building. The most memorable and powerful part of our museum tour was when the guide brought out the museum's copy of Schindler's List. It was one thing to see the list pictured on a computer while sitting at home in Canada, it was quite another see the actual list in the actual place where it was made. After visiting Gross-Rosen and thinking about my father, the power of the list became apparent. It was the ticket out of Gross-Rosen and away from certain death for my father, Hirsch Biederman, the third person listed. As the line uttered by Ben Kingsley in the movie so accurately stated: "The list was life."

We began looking through the list of names, because Rohan the director thought it would be interesting for me to point out the survivors whom I had contacted that provided me with information about my father. As I came to Albert "Bialywos" now "White," Rohan wanted me to remind the future audience of his connection to my father and how I came to contact him. Just as I was about to finish the story, the director of the museum (a short Polish middle-aged woman) interrupted and said that while we were touring the grounds she decided to look up my father in the files. She said the file confirmed that a Hirsch Biederman born on September 7, 1925 arrived in Gross-Rosen on October 16, 1944 and was given the prisoner number 68,823. I told her that he actually arrived on the fifteenth but was only officially counted, as the reader will remember, the morning of the sixteenth at the first roll call after disinfection. The prisoner number caught my attention; it was very similar to my student number at Michigan State University. It got me thinking. As I was a nineteen-year-old boy living in a dorm complaining about the food and the rooms to my father, what were his thoughts? When he was the same age he was here starving and freezing in the barracks of Gross-Rosen. I wished I could apologize to him for being so thoughtless and insensitive. Instead, I resolved that I would begin to appreciate how fortunate I was and try not to complain about small stuff anymore. Now, when things aren't going exactly my way, it often helps me to remind myself of my father and this place.

We concluded our trip to Gross-Rosen with an on-camera shoot of me summarizing what I was feeling after touring the camp. They asked me if I still believed in God. I responded that I always looked at myself as a Jew by race, not by religion. But, I said, I believe that if there is a God, my dad is a good man and would probably forgive him. For this final scene, I was filmed while seated in front of a recently installed stained glass window which depicted two prisoners in blue striped uniforms being consumed by fire.

With that, we had finished my entire story. The *Past Lives* crew members became a little emotional and were sad to see it end. It was time to head back to Wroclaw and then fly home the following morning. Rohan and I were scheduled to depart at 7:00 a.m. and after stops in Munich and then Frankfurt I would continue on to Detroit and he would go to Montreal. The rest of the crew were going on another assignment to Ireland and were scheduled to leave in the afternoon.

We arrived back in Wroclaw and the Hotel Tumski after an uneventful one-hour drive from Rogoznica. The plan was for us to take an hour break and then meet back in the lobby before heading out for a final group dinner. I went up to my room and called Randi to tell her how the day went and to remind her to pick me up the following day at Detroit Metro Airport at 4:15 p.m. She said that a horse had been dropped off at the clinic that morning (Wednesday) and she scheduled it for surgery on Friday morning. The horse was then slated to be picked up on Friday afternoon by a horse shipping company and taken to Florida for rest and recuperation over the winter months. Randi said that she only agreed to schedule the procedure because it was a short one and the owner was one of my earliest and long-time clients. She then asked if I would be up for it, so soon after my long and arduous travel itinerary. I responded that since she already scheduled the surgery, I didn't have much choice, especially since the owner already had made the arrangements to have the horse picked up that Friday afternoon.

After I hung up the phone, I wondered if Randi was a camp guard in a previous life: arranging a surgery on my first morning back home. There would be no rest for me after a transatlantic flight. Fortunately for me and the horse, it was a minimally invasive stem cell transplant procedure and he would have no problem recovering and making the ship later that day.

I was among the first veterinarians worldwide, and I believe the first in Canada, to use bone marrow derived stem cells as a standard treatment for tendon and ligament injuries in horses. Although there were initially a lot of skeptics, I had great results with the procedure. It involved removing bone marrow from a horse's sternum (breast bone) using a large biopsy needle and then injecting the material directly into an injured tendon or ligament using ultrasound guidance to locate the exact spot of the damage. There were no incisions, since everything was done with needles. Unfortunately, general anesthesia was required since we were removing bone marrow from the chest, which would be underneath the standing horse. The entire procedure took between fifteen and twenty minutes, not including induction and recovery from anesthesia. The goal of the procedure was to improve healing and significantly reduce the recuperation time required.

The techniques have improved over the years, and regenerative medicine is one of the most talked about fields of medicine today. It was nice to be one of its earliest practitioners.

After a short rest in my hotel room, I went down to the lobby and met Derek and the *Past Lives* crew for our final time together. We walked back to the Old Town and selected a restaurant. After eating, the crew wanted to explore the town. Derek and I went back to our rooms because we arranged to leave for the airport at 4:45 a.m. We both agreed that it would be best to go to bed early. Rohan, even though he was scheduled to leave in the morning with us, decided to stay with the crew.

The Trip Home

I woke up at 4:00 a.m. on Thursday, October 14 with a terrible migraine headache. It was an inauspicious start to the day. I have suffered from migraines for as long as I can remember. The severity and frequency of the headaches seems to be increasing with advancing age. I get the type of migraines in which a visual aura usually precedes the severe unrelenting pounding headache. Often the headache is accompanied by nausea and sometimes vomiting. Fortunately, the medicines available to treat migraine headaches have greatly improved in recent years. With the modern triptan class of drugs, I can *almost* go about my normal daily business after taking one, as opposed to the days before they existed. In those days I would pretty much take to my bed and suffer in severe pain for the eight to twelve hours it took for the headache to subside.

On this day, I took my medicine at 4:00 a.m. and by 4:25 the aura subsided and I was able to get dressed and finish packing. I then staggered out of my room to the elevator and down to the lobby. Derek was already there, waiting for me. So far, Rohan was a no show.

I asked Derek what was the latest time we could leave and still be on time for our flight. He advised that we leave no later than 5:00 a.m. At 4:55 I went up to Rohan's room to check on him. When I got there his door was wide open, the lights were on and the radio was blaring at full volume. As I entered the room, the scent of alcohol was overwhelming. Rohan was lying face down, passed out on top of the covers of his bed. I noticed that he was still breathing and I checked his pulse. It was strong. He didn't look like he was in any shape to fly, so I shut off his radio and lights and left him to sleep off the alcohol. When I got back to the lobby, I told the desk clerk what I discovered and left it up to her if she wanted to call EMS or not. At 5:10 a.m. Derek and I departed for the airport.

After a twenty-five-minute drive we arrived at Wroclaw international airport at 5:35 a.m. My itinerary said to be at the airport by 5:15 a.m., so apparently, I was running a little late. I said a hurried goodbye to Derek, embraced him and thanked him for everything and rushed into the airport. I was eager to observe the security and customs procedures to see if it would ever be possible, on a future trip, to take the coins out of Poland by air. As I removed my ticket from my briefcase I noticed that at the bottom of it, there were also printed instructions to arrive promptly for security check by 5:15 a.m. I was definitely arriving late. I was fortunate that there were only a few people in line ahead of me. When I came to the front of the line, the security official gave me a stern lecture about being late but then, much to my relief, directed me to the X-ray machine. After my bags were X-rayed, I was sent to the customs control table, where two customs officers were waiting: one man and one woman. Unlike the system in North America, many of the Eastern European countries require air travelers to be inspected by customs officials on exiting their country. The purpose is to determine whether the items you may have obtained while there can legally be taken out of the country. My guess was that the coins would not be among those items permitted to be removed. I always travel light and only take carry on size baggage with me. For this trip, I only took a briefcase and a small carry-on suitcase. I handed my passport to the male customs officer and laid my bags on the table in front of him. As he looked through my passport, the female officer opened my suitcase and looked through it thoroughly. I got a little nervous when the male officer stopped and hesitated for quite some time when he came to the passport page that contained my State of Israel entry stamp from a previous trip. I have often experienced this moment of hesitation whenever a foreign customs officer reaches that Israeli stamped page. As he held my passport open with his thumb on that page, he looked at me and asked if I had anything to declare. I wasn't sure what he expected me to say, so I responded that other than that I am a Jew, I have nothing else to declare. I told him that I wasn't sure, however, if it was still necessary to declare this piece of information. The officer didn't respond to my comment, although I'm sure he didn't appreciate the sarcasm. The female officer then handed my bags back to me. The man then gave me back my passport and pointed to the departure gate.

The Wroclaw airport was very small and there were only about four gates. As I took a seat at my gate, my headache began to recur. I went to the nearest concession stand, bought a coffee, and then took my second dose of migraine medicine. My day was only two hours old, and I had already taken the maximum recommended daily dose. As I sat back down at the gate, I looked out at the tarmac through the all glass terminal building and noticed the skies were getting really dark and ominous looking clouds were rolling in. I then noticed that parked in front of our gate was a Lot Polish airlines twin engine turbo prop plane, an Italian made ATR 72. I thought to myself: shit, I hope this storm holds off, because there is no way that little piece of dreck is taking off in a thunderstorm. Just as I was finishing my thoughts, the skies opened up and a torrential downpour began to fall. As boarding time approached there was no letup in the rain. I looked over at the flight monitors and suddenly all the departure times were replaced with "DELAYED." Since I only had about forty-five minutes between connecting flights, I speculated how this delay was going to affect the rest of my travels. I thought to myself: whatever happens, oh well, there's nothing I could do about it now. I then leaned back in my chair and fell into a drug induced sleep.

I was dreaming that I was in Gross-Rosen, lying on the foot path to the quarry, with an Alsatian Shepherd dog gnawing on my left arm as an SS guard stood over me; when suddenly, I was awoken by a Lot gate agent shaking me by my left arm. She said that I better hurry up if I wanted to get on my flight since they were ready to close the doors. I had slept right through the boarding announcements! I jumped up, grabbed my bags, ran to the jet way and stepped onto the plane just as the flight crew were getting ready to close the door. As I plunked myself down into my seat, I took a look at my watch; it was 9:30 a.m., two hours later than the scheduled departure time.

We arrived in Munich after the short one-hour flight from Wroclaw. When we finally came to a stop at the gate, it was 11:00 a.m. I waited impatiently for my turn to exit the plane. It's amazing how slow people seem to be moving in front of you when you are in a hurry. When I finally got off the plane, I located a monitor to see the status of my flight to Frankfurt. It was scheduled to board in five minutes. I sprinted half way across the terminal to my new departure gate. When I got there I could see out of the window and just like in Wroclaw, the skies started to darken and storms clouds rolled in. The storm had now reached Munich! Just as our boarding time came around, the skies opened up and another torrential rain began to fall. Immediately the "DELAYED" sign flashed on all the flight monitors. The stress of rushing to the gate caused my migraine to return, and I had to take my third dose of medication. I had only taken more than two doses in a single day one previous time. I took a seat at the gate and hoped the storm would pass. I tried not to fall asleep so as not to miss the boarding call. After an hour, the rain let up and the monitor showed our boarding time as 12:30 p.m. I didn't know what was going to happen to my flight to Detroit, it was scheduled to depart Frankfurt at 1:00 p.m. It was now noontime and I had been traveling for eight hours on an empty stomach, one cup of coffee, and three migraine tablets. I was hungry, nauseous, and had a headache all at the same time.

At 12:30 p.m., we boarded the Lufthansa plane and took off for Frankfurt in the now sunny weather. We arrived in Frankfurt at 1:30 p.m. After I deplaned, I hurried into the concourse and located the flight monitors. They listed my flight to Detroit as "Departed." Shit, what happens now? I asked myself. I walked over to the Detroit flight's departure gate and asked the gate agent where do I go from here? She said to go to the Lufthansa courtesy desk located in the terminal and they would make the necessary arrangements. She also said that due to the inclement weather around the country, many people had missed their connections.

I walked to the courtesy desk where there were three agents helping the one hundred plus people in line. It was really hot in the airport, and my patience was wearing thin. I was wearing my down jacket because I had no room in my suitcase for it. Aside from getting impatient, I was beginning to get overheated. Just as I got in line at the courtesy desk, two of the agents put up a closed sign on their window and walked away. "Where the fuck are you guys going?" I shouted. One of them responded that it was now two o'clock and time for their mandatory half-hour break. "Are you kidding me?" I asked. "What about all these people in line?" I added. They responded that the one agent will have to do while they take their break. "This is Germany, we have always valued our workers here, and their needs come first," one of them said. "Since when?" I responded. "What history books have you read, you asshole?" I enquired. Neither one of the agents responded as they slowly walked away.

After twenty minutes and with the line growing longer, another two agents showed up to service the progressively perturbed crowd. When I finally got to an agent, he said that I would have to stay overnight, since the next scheduled departure to Detroit was at 1:00 p.m. the following day. I told him that was unacceptable and I needed to get home that day. I asked him why they didn't hold the plane to wait for passengers who were late on connecting flights. He said it's better to have one group of late passengers than two. I asked the agent to book me on a different airline if there was one who had a flight heading to Detroit that day. He responded that he isn't authorized to do that, but they would authorize an intra-airline transfer if I could find an airline that had room and would take me. "So I'm on my own on with this?" I asked him. He responded that was their policy. I would have to get a provisional ticket from another airline and they would approve it afterwards.

I wasn't sure what the agent was talking about but went back into the concourse to check the flight monitors. I noticed that Air Canada had a flight leaving for Montreal with connections to many other smaller

Canadian cities, including Windsor, departing in thirty minutes. I walked to the opposite end of the terminal where the Air Canada gate was located and asked the gate agent about getting on that flight. She said it would be no problem since they had many seats unoccupied. I just needed Lufthansa to stamp my ticket with a transfer code and they would accept it. Easy enough, I thought. I hustled back to the Lufthansa counter and told the agent that I had found a flight. I gave him the Air Canada information. He said that he was sorry but he could not approve the transfer. "Why not?" I asked. He said that he can only approve a transfer to the exact same final destination, which in my case was Detroit. I told him that there were no other Detroit flights listed. He said he was sorry, but there was nothing he could do about it: he was only following orders. I asked to see a supervisor. The agent told me that the supervisor was on a break and I would have to wait for twenty minutes.

After the supervisor finally arrived and after a much-heated discussion, he approved my transfer to the Air Canada flight. I then sprinted across the terminal to the Air Canada gate as it was getting very close to the departure time. When I finally reached the gate, I saw the Air Canada jet taxiing away towards the runway. I had missed the flight. "Son of a bitch," I said to myself.

At that point I decided to call Randi to let her know that I definitely wouldn't be on the Detroit flight and I would give her more information when I figured out what I was doing. To my chagrin, neither my Polish nor Canadian cell phones would work in Germany. As I sat swearing at my phones, an Air Canada gate agent overheard me and offered me the services of her cell phone. Her cell phone worked; I was able to call Randi and tell her to sit tight and I would let her know when and where I would be arriving.

I then went back to the concourse to check out potential departing flights. There was another Air Canada flight departing at 6:00 p.m., three hours from the present time, destined for Toronto with a short stopover in Montreal.

I went to the Air Canada gate and asked if there was any availability on that flight. The agent said the plane was only half full and it would be no problem for me to get a seat. I then asked her if there were any flights connecting to Windsor from Toronto. She said there was one last flight leaving Toronto for Windsor after this flight had arrived. I asked her to book me through to Windsor and then I would see what my friends at Lufthansa would have to say.

With a provisional Canadian boarding pass in hand, I went back to the Lufthansa counter. When I showed the agent my Canadian itinerary he immediately approved it. I was quite shocked. He re-stamped my Lufthansa ticket with a new transfer number and with that I was booked. It was official! I was going home! I was scheduled to arrive at Windsor airport shortly after midnight, local time. It actually worked out pretty well since Windsor airport was only about five miles from my home.

I asked the Lufthansa agent if he had a phone I could use to call my wife and let her know of my new travel plans. He said company policy does not allow any outgoing calls. Since I already had my authorized ticket in hand, I told him to drop dead and screw his airline, his rules, and his country. I then walked away from the Lufthansa desk for the very last time.

I stopped by a concession stand and bought a bagel with cream cheese and a coffee. I then went to the Air Canada section and asked an agent if I could call my wife. She gladly handed me her cell phone. I told Randi I would call her when I touched down in Windsor. As I sat down my head began pounding. I took my fourth migraine pill of the day with my food, then found a bench in a quiet corner of the terminal, stretched out across it, and fell asleep.

I woke up in plenty of time to board the Air Canada flight to Toronto. The gate agent told me that this was the last ever flight for this particular plane. It was a Boeing 747, and Air Canada was removing them from their fleet. They were huge gas guzzlers and had become too expensive to operate. After this one was retired, they had one left, and it was due to be mothballed at the end of the month. I was given a bulkhead seat right across from one of the flight attendants.

While we were waiting to take off, I started to get aura again and took my fifth migraine pill of the day. I had now used the entire supply I brought to Poland with me in one day. The flight attendant, upon seeing me taking the medication, said that she also suffers from severe migraines. She added that, unfortunately, her next flight was to Hawaii, and Hawaii was the migraine center of the world. I had never heard that before, and asked her if she was joking. She said that it is well known that migraine sufferers have a significant increase in the likelihood of a migraine when in Hawaii. It was the first time I had ever heard such a thing. Oddly enough, in the closing segment of the *Past Lives* show, when the producer asked me what comes next, I responded that I was going to take a break from the Holocaust studies and take my wife to Hawaii. She had been patiently waiting for many years and many trips through concentration camps and Jewish cemeteries to go there. Now I wasn't so sure. Who needs to fly somewhere and be sick like this again?

In the number of years since that flight, I have only heard one other person mention migraines and Hawaii. It was enough, however, to prevent me from going there to this day.

As soon as the plane started moving, I got very dizzy and vomited. The flight attendant brought me a bag of ice for my head and, as I laid back awaiting takeoff and then the long flight home, I was reminded of the story of my parents' journey to America…

April 1949, and Beyond: The American Journey

On April 16, 1949, Hirsch and Sally woke up early and each packed up their meager belongings into the single suitcase that was permitted for each passenger travelling to America. Sally was excited about her move to America but also somewhat scared. There was also a touch of sadness as she noticed her dog Jokusz nervously watching the preparations. She wondered if he knew that soon he would have a new family and would never see her or Hirsch again.

After they were finished packing, Hirsch put all their necessary documents into a briefcase along with their entire life savings of three hundred dollars. It was now time to leave. They locked the door to their unit and walked to the administration building and turned in their key. Waiting out front, at the pre-arranged time, to drive them to the train station was their Austrian friend, Ed Guenther. Ed was a Linz native and an aide worker at the DP camp. Ed was also going to take Jokusz home with him after Sally and Hirsch had departed.

Sally, Hirsch and Jokusz got into Ed's car and headed off for the Linz train station. It was only a short drive from Bindermichl.

Before going to the station, they made a stop at the St. Barbara Friedhof cemetery which was located less than a mile away from the station. Sally, Hirsch and Ed got out and left Jokusz in the car after they parked on the street in front of the cemetery. Together they walked to the grave of Sally's mother Felicja, who had died five months previously.

When they reached the gravesite, Sally kneeled down and kissed the headstone over the spot where Felicja's name was engraved. She began to cry uncontrollably as Hirsch and Ed each placed a small stone on the headstone in accordance with Jewish tradition upon visiting a grave. After a few minutes, Ed and Hirsch got on either side of Sally and both gently helped her to her feet. After Sally said one final goodbye to her mother, the three of them then walked out of the cemetery to Ed's vehicle. It was to be the last time Hirsch or Sally would ever visit Felicja's gravesite.

After a short drive, they arrived at the Linz train station. Hirsch and Sally embraced Ed and told him to take good care of Jokusz. Before Sally got out of the car, she kissed Jokusz on the forehead. Hirsch and Sally then grabbed their suitcases from the trunk and, after shutting it, watched as Ed drove off. Sally cried as she saw Jokusz looking longingly at them through the passenger window as he was driven away.

For many years after coming to America, Sally continued to correspond with Ed until the end of his life. Ed took care of Jokusz for the remainder of the dog's life. Ed also sent Sally a picture of her mother's grave and placed flowers at it annually, on the anniversary of her death. This was a great comfort to Sally.

After a ten-hour train ride from Linz, Hirsch and Sally arrived at Bremerhaven. They took a bus to the dock and then checked into the designated hostel for passengers of the *General Hersey*.

The following morning, they went to the US immigration station and reported for their final inspections. After Hirsch gave his name to the immigration officer, the officer responded: "You are going to America now, that name won't do. It sounds too much like *hearse*, you know, the car they drive caskets in. My grandfather's name is Harry, why don't we call you Harry." Hirsch shrugged in agreement as the officer wrote down Harry Biederman on the ship's roster. From now on, Hirsch would be forever known in America as "Harry."

Harry and Sally then went through the mandatory medical exam and psychiatric evaluation. This was followed by one final interview in which they were again asked if they were Nazis, Communists, or war criminals. After they confirmed that they weren't, Sally and Harry were allowed to board the former troop ship, the USS *General Hersey*.

As they boarded the ship, they were given their berth assignments. The *General Hersey* was still configured as a troop ship and thus the passenger decks consisted of several compartments of canvas bunks stacked five high. The men were kept separate from the women. Children were bunked in with their mothers. Each bunk was approximately six-feet long by three-feet wide. Each compartment shared a shower, sink, and toilet. For the next eleven days this would be home for Harry and Sally.

In the late afternoon of April 17, 1949 the *General Hersey* departed Bremerhaven. Harry and Sally watched from the top deck as Europe slowly disappeared forever into the background.

As soon as the ship hit the open seas, the water became choppy and many passengers became seasick. Sally was among them. She spent the first hour on the top deck vomiting over the stern railing.

Sally never got over her seasickness and, in fact, both she and Harry spent much of the next ten days either vomiting over the sides of the top deck of the ship or in the toilet of their compartments.

Finally, in the early morning of Thursday, April 28 they had reached New York Harbor. All of the passengers rushed to the top deck to catch a glimpse of the Statue of Liberty. Harry and Sally were in awe as the Manhattan skyline came into view. They were ready and excited to start their new lives in America.

Sally and Harry were further amazed by the majesty of the Brooklyn Bridge as the big ship passed under it before steaming into port and docking at the Brooklyn Navy Yard. After eleven miserable days at sea, their ship had finally come in. Harry and Sally watched excitedly as the gangplank was extended to shore. When they walked across it, they were now in America, there was no turning back; Europe was nothing but a distant, terrible memory.

After completing some paperwork, they picked up their suitcases and were directed to a bus that was waiting to take them to Grand Central Station in Midtown Manhattan, which was where Sally had prearranged to meet her "Aunt" Sarah. Sally had never met Sarah before and she was hoping that they would recognize each other from the photographs they had exchanged.

Sarah was actually Sally's mother's first cousin. She was born in Poland in 1894 but was sent to live with relatives in America after she was orphaned at six years old. Her mother had died when she was five, and her father passed away one year later. In 1916 Sarah married a Jewish man from Brooklyn. Soon after they were married, he was drafted as an infantryman into the US army and shipped to France after the United States entered World War I. In 1918, he was killed in action. Sarah never remarried and had been living on her army widow's pension for the past thirty years. Sarah agreed to sponsor Sally and Harry for immigration to the United States and then in America until they could get on their own feet. After World War II, it was a very difficult process for displaced persons to find a country to accept them. Harry and Sally put in applications to immigrate to a few countries once they arrived in Bindermichl. Having an American sponsor greatly expedited the approval of their green card application.

After Harry and Sally got off the bus and retrieved their suitcases, they walked over to the agreed on meeting place inside Grand Central station.

Although Harry had never met Sarah, he had seen pictures of her and immediately recognized her by her drooping left eyelid, a condition she acquired at birth when she suffered nerve damage during a difficult labor and delivery. They exchanged hugs and then began to walk to the subway station located across 42nd Street that would take them to Sarah's Lower East Side tenement.

When Harry and Sally exited Grand Central station, the first thing they saw was the adjacent art deco styled Chrysler building. As they then turned to look south, they saw the iconic Empire State Building, with its spire reaching skyward, only eight blocks away. They were both awestruck by what they were seeing. It took their breath away. They were amazed at the city that was now their new home.

It was only a short subway ride to Sarah's Orchard Street tenement. When they emerged from the nearest station, Harry could not believe what he was seeing. He felt as if he had fallen into the abyss. On either side of the streets were grimy, soot covered dilapidated brick tenement buildings. Each one had various types of tattered clothing hanging from clotheslines strung across the external wrought iron balconies and stairways which were supposed to be used as fire escapes. There was also garbage everywhere. The streets and alleyways and fire escapes were all overflowing with foul smelling trash. In the streets, kids with dirty faces wearing dirty clothes, some without shoes, were playing a strange game which consisted of hitting a ball with a stick and then running after it. Had these kids never heard of football (soccer), Harry wondered? He could not believe that such a place could exist, just a short ride away from the wonders of Midtown Manhattan. This was worse than any neighborhood that he had seen in Europe. It was certainly a step down from Bindermichl.

When they reached Sarah's building, the surroundings would only get worse. After entering the building, they climbed the stairs up to the fourth floor. On each floor, there were four individual units accessible through a narrow hallway. All four units shared a common lavatory consisting of two toilets; there were no faucets or sinks. As Sarah opened the door to her unit Harry was shocked by its appearance. As he entered, a narrow hallway took him past two small bedrooms and then into a small sitting room that was continuous with the makeshift kitchen/washroom. In the kitchen there was a sink and adjacent cast iron bathtub underneath a bank of rotting wooden cabinets. Covering the tub was a wooden plank which doubled as the kitchen counter. Sarah explained that after preparing dinner the plank is removed, and the tub becomes accessible for bathing. Next to the tub was a small gas stove and oven. Also in the kitchen was a tiny two-person table.

The entire living area was less than five hundred square feet. Sarah gave Sally and Harry the slightly larger of the two bedrooms, although it did not matter since each one was only equipped with a single twin size bed.

After viewing the house, Sally and Harry were both despondent. Harry told Sally that he was ready to go back to Austria; there was no way he was going to live like this. Sally tried to calm him down and told him that when she goes to work at her new job at the Jewish Welfare Federation on Monday, she would try to make other accommodations. (Both Harry and Sally had jobs prearranged for them in New York by the American Joint Distribution Committee while they were still in Austria). Harry agreed to stick out the weekend, but if something wasn't done soon, he was going back to Austria. This was terrible.

On Monday morning May 2, Sally reported to work at the Jewish Welfare Federation office in Manhattan. She immediately told them to send her somewhere else because she couldn't stay in New York and live in these awful conditions. Her new supervisor at the Federation told her that there was an opening coming up in the Detroit office starting on June 1. He also said that they could arrange employment for her husband, Harry, at the Ford Highland Park assembly plant. The supervisor also informed her of an opening in the Providence, Rhode Island office, giving her the option to go there instead of Detroit. Sally responded that she didn't care where she and Harry were sent as long as there were opportunities for them to both work hard and make a good living. Ultimately the supervisor decided to send them to Detroit.

On May 25, 1949; Harry and Sally packed their bags and said good-bye to "Aunt" Sarah. They would not see Sarah again until they returned to New York to attend a wedding in July 1971. She was suffering from cancer at that time and died a few years later. They were informed of her death by the Jewish Benevolent Society in New York when the Society was seeking next of kin to cover the funeral costs. My mother paid for Sarah's interment. I don't know why they did not stay in closer touch after Harry and Sally left for Detroit. Perhaps Sarah was offended at their abrupt departure. I never thought of asking my mother about it… and unfortunately it is too late now.

Harry and Sally headed back to New York's Grand Central Station, and soon they were aboard a train bound for Detroit. In Detroit, they were assigned a duplex on Richton Street with their rent paid by the Jewish Welfare Federation for three months. Afterwards, they would be responsible for paying the rent on their own. The duplex was located just a few blocks from the Highland Park Ford Assembly plant and also a few blocks from the Dexter and Davison Street intersection which was the main hub of Jewish life in Detroit.

Harry and Sally immediately fell in love with Detroit. Their neighborhood was home to many other Holocaust Survivors, and they immediately made lots of friends. There was also a vibrant Jewish cultural scene in Detroit with almost nightly activities.

At the Detroit Jewish Welfare Federation, Sally became the office manager within a short period of time. Harry worked at the Ford plant for three months and decided assembly line work was not for him. He answered an ad and took a job working for a lighting store repairing lamps and fixtures. Harry was very skilled and was able to complete all the repairs in a very short time. He sat around idly for most of the day. There wasn't enough work to keep him busy.

The owner of the store, Max Friedman, had a cousin who was an electrical contractor. One day the cousin mentioned to Max that he was looking for a new electrician. Max knew just the man. He asked Harry if he wanted to work as an electrician full time and fix the lamps in his spare time. He could take the lamps home and work on them in the evenings or on weekends. Harry jumped at the opportunity.

After getting his new job, Harry and Sally moved to a larger duplex on Buena Vista Street, just a few blocks away. After a short apprenticeship with his new company, Harry passed the electrical licensing exam and became a licensed journeyman electrician. Harry was a much sought-after electrician and from 1951 to 1955 he was recruited by several contracting firms. As a skilled hard-working electrician, he was offered many jobs and was able to select the best ones. In the four years that had elapsed since he became a licensed electrician, he had worked for multiple contracting companies. This enabled him to experience a variety of management techniques.

In 1955, Harry and Sally again moved to a larger home on Tyler Street a few blocks north of their current home on Buena Vista. In the summer of 1955 Harry injured his back when he fell from a wooden step ladder after it snapped at its base. During the three months he was off recovering, he took a course to upgrade his status from journeyman to master electrician. This was a necessary step if he wanted to open his own business, since only master electricians could take out municipal electrical permits. Early in 1956, Harry passed the Licensing test and became a licensed master electrician. Shortly afterwards the Harry Biederman Electric Company was founded. It was a joint effort with Sally. After she would finish work at the Jewish Federation she would come home, make dinner and then manage the books at night. She was in charge of managing the payroll, billing, and accounts payable and receivable.

After two years in business they bought their first home on Avon Street in the predominantly Jewish suburb of Oak Park. Not long afterward, after thirteen years of marriage, Sally became pregnant and in 1959, gave birth to their first child, a son they named Edward. Sally planned on working at the Jewish Federation until Edward was born but had to go on maternity leave early when she became quite ill during her pregnancy. After Edward was born, Sally became a stay at home mom and manager of the family business. I was born twenty-one months after Edward.

Back Home: Ontario, 2004

Shortly after 10:00 p.m., and after the ten-hour flight from Frankfurt with a short stopover in Montreal, the Air Canada 747 that I was aboard made its final landing at Pearson International airport in Toronto. I was sick the entire journey. I again thought about my parents, and I wondered: although neither of them ever suffered from migraine headaches, how did they survive the seasickness and accompanying nausea for eleven days during their transatlantic journey. The more I thought about it, the more aware I became of how difficult every aspect of their life had been. I became more impressed with their toughness and fortitude.

As I got up to exit the aircraft, the flight attendant sitting across from me noticed my unsteadiness. Being a fellow migraine sufferer, she understood the dizziness and visual disturbances that I was experiencing. She asked me if I had a connecting flight or if Toronto was my final destination. When I told her that I was connecting to Windsor and I only had a half an hour to get to my gate, she kindly offered to escort me there. I was grateful for the assistance because by this time I could barely see. It was now twenty-four hours, and four flights later, since I had awoken with a severe unrelenting migraine in Wroclaw.

I made it to my gate on time and took off for Windsor at 11:00 p.m. During the short one-hour flight, my thoughts again turned to my parents. I thought about all they had accomplished and wondered how they did it. I wondered if, during the period before I was born, they had all the same problems that I witnessed as a kid. Was there the insomnia, the nightmares, the prescription drug dependency, the alcoholism? Or perhaps did some of that come later with success and the associated leisure time that success offered. I decided that when I recovered from this journey, I would look a little deeper into their lives in the 1950s during that period before I was born. I wondered if my father ever thought about the coins that were still buried in that ceramic teapot in the backyard of the home on Zeglarska Street in Lodz.

Shortly past midnight on Friday, October 15 we landed in Windsor. I haven't had a lot of occasions to fly Air Canada in the ensuing years since that day, but I must say, I was extremely grateful for the assistance and service the staff and crew provided to me on my difficult journey home. When I got off the plane, Randi was there at the gate eagerly waiting for my arrival. When she saw the state I was in, she whisked me out to the car and then, after the short drive home, I quickly undressed and collapsed into my bed. Somehow, I was able to wake up eight hours later and perform the scheduled surgery flawlessly. Maybe I picked up some of my parents' work ethic and toughness? I saw a few more patients that day and then went home and collapsed into my bed, which is where I spent most of the weekend.

On Friday, October 22, after my headaches had abated and I was back to my normal clinical routine, I finally received by mail the much anticipated package from Joanna Podolska. It was a manila envelope and was heavily sealed with packaging tape. Although I was eager to view the information contained within, I knew that if my father's sisters' birth certificates were enclosed and I was able to now put names to the murdered girls' faces, the tragedy would become much more personal. After fumbling with a knife due to my nervous anticipation, I was finally able to get the envelope opened. I could almost picture Joanna back in her office in Lodz laughing and saying "Did you think I was going to make it that easy for you?"

Polish magazine featuring my story.

Once I was able to open the envelope, I emptied the contents onto my desk. Among the items included were the May 7, 2004 *Lodz Gazette*, which featured the story about my father's family and the coins, the World War II magazine for which I was interviewed in Warsaw, birth certificates of my father's three sisters, and a marriage certificate for my father's parents.

As I laid the documents side-by-side, I was overcome with emotion. Twenty years had now elapsed since I had inadvertently located the mysterious photos of four unidentified children in a drawer in my deceased father's nightstand. After four grueling trips to Poland, thousands of hours of study, hundreds of trips to libraries and archives around the world, and dozens of survivors interviewed, I had finally made good on that twenty-year-old vow

My father's sisters' birth certificates and my grandparent's marriage certificate.

that I had made to my mother and to myself. As promised, I had found my father's family coin collection, discovered the names, birth dates, and *yahrzeit* (memorial) dates of his sisters (the children in the pictures) and parents, and, lastly, I had learned where and how they were "killed by the Germans."

My father's oldest sister was named Tzipora. This was a common girl's name in Eastern European Jewish families. It is a Hebrew name and translates to "little songbird" in English. She was born on January 28, 1913 in Lodz. At the age of twenty-nine, on August 10, 1942 she was killed by a gunshot to the head from a German military issued carbine rifle and buried in a mass grave, along with her mother and sister, in the old Jewish cemetery in Krosno. It is uncertain, although likely, that this was done while my father was forced to witness.

The next eldest Biederman sister was named Pesha. This was also a very common girl's name among Jews in Eastern Europe. Pesha is the Yiddish equivalent of the Biblical Hebrew name "Batya." It is translated to English as "Daughter of God." She was born on May 18, 1914, also in Lodz. On August 10, 1942 at the age of twenty-eight, this Daughter of God was also killed by a rifle shot to the head and buried with her sister and mother in a mass grave in the Jewish cemetery in Krosno.

My father's youngest sister was named Sara. Sara of course was the name of Abraham's wife in the Bible. It is the most common Jewish girl's name in the world. Sara is translated to English as "princess." She was born in Lodz on March 3, 1920 and was five years older than my father. On August 10, 1942 she was taken by rail from Krosno to the extermination camp in Belzec. At the age of twenty-two she was killed, along with her father, by asphyxiation of diesel exhaust while locked in an air tight chamber with hundreds other Jews. Her remains were incinerated and buried in former farmland around the camp perimeter.

My father's mother was named Esther Malka Biederman. Her maiden name was Lewkowicz. Her dual first name is from the Purim story in the Bible and is translated as "Queen Esther." She was born in 1886 (the date was not specified in the marriage certificate) in Lodz, Poland and was married to Lipa (Leopold) on September 13, 1911. At the age of fifty-six she was shot and killed, along with her two eldest daughters at the Jewish cemetery in Krosno and also buried in a mass grave on that dark August 10 day in 1942.

Esther's husband, Lipa, was born in Opatowiec, Poland which is in the Galicia region and ironically not far from Krosno, the site of his eventual deportation in December 1939. Like his wife, he was also born sometime in 1886. He was around fifty-six years old when he was asphyxiated along with his youngest daughter in the extermination camp in Belzec, Poland on

August 10, 1942. His remains are also scattered in a farmer's field in Belzec, Poland.

When I received my paternal grandparent's marriage certificate, I was surprised to learn that my father's father Lipa was not from Lodz. It seems his family moved there from Opatowiec, Poland sometime before he met Esther, his future wife. The marriage certificate also confirmed that my father's grandfather and Lipa's father was indeed the Saul Biederman whose grave I visited in the Lodz old Jewish cemetery. The fact that Saul moved from Opatowiec explained why I was unable to find many other Biedermans buried in the Lodz cemetery. Saul was the first Biederman in my father's family and, ironically, the only one, to die and be buried in Lodz. I'm guessing that Saul's wife either died in Opatowiec or is buried in Lodz under her maiden name. In the marriage certificate, both the bride's and groom's mothers are listed by their maiden names. They may not have adopted their husband's surnames. I haven't been back to Poland since I received Joanna's letter to check that out.

I was also interested to discover my own biased perspective. Because of our male dominated society, it never occurred to me in my early research that the mattress factory owner may have been from my father's mother's side of the family. In that case, I should have looked up the Lewkowicz Mattress Factory in the Polish phone book when I went to the New York Public Library. Unfortunately, I only learned the name Lewkowicz with the arrival of this marriage certificate. It also seems likely that the coins came to Lodz from the Netherlands with the Lewkowicz family and that my paternal grandfather, Lipa Biederman, was the fortunate son-in-law. Maybe that's why my father told me that if I always worked hard I would succeed, but marrying a rich girl, he added, doesn't hurt either.

Another piece of information that I learned from the birth certificates which I received from Joanna, aside from my father's sisters' names, was their ages. Because the only photographs I had of these girls were from when they were children, it hadn't really occurred to me that they were actually adult women when they were killed.

Under normal circumstances, most Eastern European Jewish girls of their ages would have been married. It is obvious, however, that once the war started and their lives were in utter turmoil, the last thing on those girls' minds would be getting married. For them, it was a struggle just to survive on a daily basis. When they were ultimately killed on August 10, 1942 not only did the Germans take away three potential aunts, they also took along with them any future cousins that may have attended that first birthday party of mine. It was at that birthday party that I first noticed the absence which started me on this entire journey.

Late 2004–Present: Epilogue

The weekend after receiving the magazine and newspaper from Joanna, I took them to my mother's home so that she could help me translate them into English. When I walked into her foyer, I noticed something that immediately caught my attention. Hanging in the foyer was a twelve-year-old framed lithograph that my mother purchased at a Hadassah charity auction in 1992. I had seen it hundreds of times before and never really paid much attention to it. Across the bottom of the artwork was the title "1492–1992 commemorating 500 years since the Spanish expulsion." The artwork depicted Jews leaving Spain by many different routes and ending up in five main destinations. One of them was the Netherlands. It suddenly occurred to me that this former meaningless piece of art was now depicting part of my family history. If it wasn't for my visit to the Lodz Museum where I learned that some of my family came to Lodz from the Netherlands, I would have never known that the Lewkowicz family, like most Dutch Jews, were originally Sephardic Jews from Spain; and that the lithograph would have remained forever meaningless. Today it hangs in my foyer in Laguna Beach, California.

In the world today, there are two main subcultures of Jews: Sephardic and Ashkenazic. Ashkenazic Jews are the Jews of Central or Eastern European ancestry and Sephardic Jews are of Spanish, North African, or Middle Eastern descent. Each subgroup has their own set of customs, traditions, foods, and language. Although both groups pray in the holy language of Hebrew, each has a different language for daily conversational use. The Ashkenazis speak Yiddish (a hybrid of German and Hebrew) while the Sephardics speak Ladino (a hybrid of Spanish and Hebrew).

The Sephardics are descended from Jews who lived on the Iberian peninsula of Spain around 1000 AD. Sephardic in Hebrew means Spanish. Sephardic Jews were those Iberian Jews who disagreed with certain mainstream rabbinical decrees and interpretations and divided into their own sect. They have a slightly different pronunciation of Hebrew and also have their own interpretation of Jewish law.

In 1492, near the end of the Spanish Inquisition, the Catholic monarchs of a divided Spain, Queen Isabella and King Ferdinand, issued an edict that has come to be known as the Edict of Alhambra. It decreed that all people living in Spain must convert to Catholicism or be expelled. The Sephardic Jewish Lewkowicz family made the fateful decision to keep the faith of their ancient religion and leave Spain. Had they converted to Catholicism, they would have been allowed to remain in Spain and live in peace with the equal rights of any other good Christians, albeit carefully monitored to ensure that they did not secretly continue with their Jewish faith. Four hundred and fifty years later another Catholic dictator (Adolf Hitler) would come to power, but this Bavarian one would offer them no such option of conversion. Because of the decision made by Señor Lewkowicz in 1492, future generations would continue to be recognized as Jews, regardless of what they believed, and in the end that desire to remain Jews would lead the Lewkowicz family into near extinction.

After I recovered from the excitement of discovering the lithograph and its relevance to my family history, I sat down with my mother and went over the newspaper and magazine articles that I brought with me.

After translating the articles to English, she said to me: "These are nice stories but I don't think they are your father's coins."

"Are you kidding me? You still aren't convinced that dad was from Lodz? What about all the birth certificates and the marriage certificate?" I replied.

"How much did the Polish reporter charge you for the birth certificates?" asked my mother.

"She didn't charge me," I replied. "She wanted them for her own interest and for the story. What makes you think she would charge me for them?" I enquired.

"Because they're fake," my mother replied. "She just wanted to take money from you," she added.

I decided not to argue. Sooner or later, I thought that my mother, being an intelligent woman, would realize that it was obviously irrefutable that my father was from Lodz and his family buried the coins.

Although I would've liked it to happen sooner, finally in 2012, shortly before her death, my mother conceded to me that indeed my father was from Lodz and the coins were his. At that time, she was in the hospital being visited by one of the staff clergymen when I also arrived to visit. She introduced me to the attending Rabbi as her son, the famous veterinarian and archaeologist. She went on to list my medical accomplishments and my finding the coins.

After recovering from the shock of her admission, I began to wonder: had she accepted the facts of my research all along? I wondered if it was because she never got over her anger at me for traveling to Poland against her wishes that she refused to give me any credit for my discovery. I wasn't really sure what she believed and never did get the chance to find out. On that particular day, I didn't want to further question her with the Rabbi being present, so I decided to drop the subject. I was happy to leave it where it was. Ultimately, I was never able to determine what my mother truly believed; she died shortly after that visit.

Back in her living room in 2004, I decided to drop the subject of Lodz and the coins. Besides having the two articles translated, I wanted to look into my parents' lives and mental states in the 1950s. It was a difficult subject to discuss with my mother, so I decided to rely on her Wiedergutmachung files. I remembered seeing some medical notes back when I skimmed through the file in the fall of 2003. I took the Wiedergutmachung files home with me in the old shoebox where my mother had stowed them nearly forty years earlier and began my research.

In 1951, the Conference of Jewish Material Claims against Germany was established in New York. The conference consisted of a number of Jewish national and international organizations and its stated aim was to obtain funds for relief and rehabilitation and indemnification for injuries inflicted on victims of Nazi persecution.

The conference was assembled by the government of the State of Israel which claimed it had the right to seek reparations for the relief and resettlement of Jewish victims of Nazi persecution. On the Jewish holiday of Rosh Hashanah in 1951, West German Chancellor Konrad Adenauer invited the conference and the State of Israel to negotiate when he said in a speech: "unspeakable crimes were perpetrated in the name of the German people, which impose upon them the obligation to make moral and material amends."

In March of 1952, the negotiations began in The Hague and later that year an agreement was signed in Luxembourg between the state of Israel, the conference, and the German government. The agreement called for the West German government to provide compensation and restitution to Holocaust survivors. The East German communist government claimed that they were anti-fascist throughout the war and therefore were not liable for the crimes committed by the Nazis.

Beginning in 1953 and continuing well into the 1960s the West German government passed a series of laws known as the Federal Indemnification Laws which established the framework of how the victims of Nazi persecution would be compensated. These became known as the Wiedergutmachung laws. The laws established strict guidelines for compensation to eligible Holocaust survivors. Under the new laws, some survivors were eligible to receive one-time restitution payments; others were eligible to receive one-time payments plus monthly pensions. Survivors were also eligible to claim a reimbursement for medical expenses incurred from a "recognized" illness. A recognized illness was one which was determined to be the direct result of Nazi persecution. Survivors were also eligible to receive an increase in their monthly pension for deterioration of their condition due to the recognized illness. These laws remained in effect after German re-unification in 1991.

As a result of the above agreement, beginning in 1953 and continuing for the next fifteen years, my parents were in constant litigation with the German government over their restitution cases. During that time they were examined by German or German approved doctors and psychiatrists to determine their eligibility for certain types of compensation.

After reading through the many documents, I was able to determine the reparations made to my parents and also was able to put together a pretty good picture of their health and state of mind in the 1950s and 1960s.

The first portion of restitution that my parents received was for forced labor during the time they spent detained in the various concentration camps. In order to receive this compensation, they had to submit a list of the dates and times spent in each camp. Although the Germans had most of these records already, they still made each survivor recount the details on their own. Any discrepancy between the survivors' memories and the German's records resulted in a denial of the claim. The survivor then had to re-file the claim with the corrected dates in order to finally receive their compensation.

For the first portion of restitution my mother received a onetime payment of 12,600 Deutsche Marks for four years and twenty-six days of incarceration in concentration camps. This was equivalent to 3,150 dollars or 770 dollars per year of incarceration.

My father spent three years and twenty-two days incarcerated in concentration camps and was awarded a onetime payment of 8,400 Deutsche Marks or 2,100 dollars. For restitution purposes, Schindler's factory was considered to be a concentration camp.

The second portion of restitution my parents received was for forced labor and confinement in their various ghettos. My mother spent sixteen months and twenty-seven days in the Krakow Ghetto and was compensated a onetime payment of 2,400 Deutsche Marks or approximately 600 dollars. My father was confined to his home in Lodz and then the Krosno Ghetto and Airbase for thirty-three months and twenty days. He received a onetime payment of 4,950 Deutsche Marks or approximately 1,235 dollars.

In total, my mother spent five years, four months and fifty-three days, basically her entire teenage years, enslaved and brutalized by the Nazis. My father's total was five years, nine months and forty-two days. Although my parents' murdered family members were also incarcerated and performed years of slave labor prior to being murdered, my parents received no compensation whatsoever for them or the slave they labor performed.

The final phase of restitution my parents were awarded was a monthly pension and reimbursement for ongoing medical expenses. The monthly pension was based on their level of disability and relied heavily on their medical history and the results of German approved doctors' evaluations. I found two letters in my father's file which basically summed up both of my parents' conditions.

The first letter was one where my father explained his physical disabilities incurred while a concentration camp inmate. In this letter he referred to the previously mentioned incident at the Gross-Rosen Concentration Camp where he had to stand overnight in the freezing rain on the *appelplatz*. As a result of this, he later suffered frostbite and pneumonia.

Both of my parents' mental conditions were summed up by the second letter. It was written by a German approved physician and summarized the results of his medical evaluation. The letter was sent to the German restitution office as part of my father's pension claim. It read as follows:

This man suffers from chronic bronchitis, severe mental and emotional trauma and has all the classic side effects from his years of incarceration as a victim of the Nazis.

His chief complaints at this time and for the past 12 to 14 years has been insomnia, horror nightmares, inability to concentrate at times, shortness of breath and recurrent upper respiratory infections due to his chronic bronchitis. He further complains of vertigo and has episodes of weakness.

In my opinion, the traumatic experience of this man's imprisonment in a concentration camp during the last world war has caused irrevocable damage to his mental and emotional make-up. Therefore his physical symptoms may never be completely alleviated.

When I was looking through my parent's requests for reimbursement of medical expenses, I didn't find any for my father. It seems that he avoided doctors and instead self-medicated with alcohol. I remembered that when I was a kid, my father would say how much he hated and distrusted doctors.

My mother, on the other hand, was under constant psychiatric care and became heavily dependent on powerful anti-depressant and anti-psychotic drugs. Many of these drugs that were prescribed had side effects which weren't clearly understood in the 1950s when they first began being used.

It was into this environment that I was born in 1961. Somehow, despite their problems, my father and mother managed to start an electrical business and became very successful while also raising two boys. After reading the Wiedergutmachung file, I still don't know how they were able to do it.

When I finished my review of the Wiedergutmachung file I was stunned at the paltry sum that Holocaust survivors received. From what I remember, my parents' monthly pension in the 1970s was around four hundred dollars. My father's payments ceased when he died in 1981. My mother's payments increased over the years and in the final months before she died in 2012, she was receiving about two thousand dollars per month.

I remember asking my mother in 2004 if the pension was worth all the trouble. Was it really worth going through all the years of legal wrangling and having to recall all the terrible memories of the camps and the murder of her family at just the time when she was trying to put it behind her and try to live a normal life? Why did she do it? I asked. By the time the compensation began, she and my father were already very successful with the electrical business.

Her answer has stuck with me until today and has reminded me how, despite all her problems, she was among the most intelligent and insightful persons I have ever known.

"The Wiedergutmachung case wasn't about the money," my mother explained. "The money was bupkes," (meaningless) she said. "This was about putting everything on the record and getting the Germans to document and admit to their crimes. Because one day," my mother said, "some anti-Semite will come along and say all this was just a bunch of Jewish lies and conspiracy to destroy the German nation and advance the Jewish agenda. They will say the Holocaust never happened," she said. "Eventually this shoebox full of records will be yours and it will be your responsibility to respond."

As I thought about my mother's rather profound observation about the money she received in the Wiedergutmachung case, I began to think about my own situation and the coins. I was beginning to look at them in much the same way. They were material objects with a finite value; the information that I had discovered and documented was the real value of this long quest. The knowledge and understanding I gained about my parents (and myself in the process) was priceless.

Consequently, I decided that, for the time being, the coins would remain where they were: in a showcase in Poland. At that point in my life, after the odyssey that was my last trip home, there was no way I was ready to face another journey to the depressing place that is Lodz, Poland. It was time to return to my life as a full-time horse veterinarian.

On November 15, 2004, my episode of *Past Lives* was aired on Global TV in Canada for the first time. I thought the show was well done but I was disappointed at how much film footage was omitted to make the final half hour long (commercials included) television show. This was my first time being involved in a television production, and I didn't realize how little of the actual filming ends up in the finished product. We filmed from eight to ten hours a day for almost two weeks and ended up with about twenty-six minutes of airtime. Despite my disappointment, however, my episode was the highest rated *Past Lives* show ever. In fact, my episode attracted more viewers than all of the other *Past Lives* episodes added together. This served as an example of the enormous interest that still exists in the Holocaust and Holocaust related stories. As I stated earlier, even though I was initially disappointed after watching the show, in the end I was extremely gratified when I learned of the successful ratings. It made the memory of my horrible flight home a lot easier to accept.

In 2005, we moved my mother from her condominium into an assisted living facility. When I was emptying her condo, I came across several hidden stashes of small amounts of cash and other valuables. I remembered that this was also the case when we moved her out of our family home in 1984 after my father died. Only at that time it was my father who had hidden the money. It seems that my parents never recovered from the memories of the Nazis rounding them up and removing them from their homes. I believe that both of them thought it could happen again, even in America. To the average North American this may seem like paranoia, but to them the fear was justified and very real. Only this time they would be ready. Even if their bank accounts were seized, they would have enough cash to buy safe passage to somewhere, most likely Israel. I know it is difficult for the average American to understand, but this is the reason for the almost fanatical support for the State of Israel among Jews of my parents and my generation. Unlike in 1939, this time we would have a place of refuge.

As I was amassing the various caches of cash and jewelry a thought suddenly hit me like a lightning bolt. Did my father and grandfather also hide their valuables in multiple locations in their backyard? Is there more stuff buried on Zeglarska Street? I thought about what Joanna had told me about the day that Yaron unearthed the coins: how he had scanned the entire property and found them in one last desperate final attempt, but could there be more?

I realized that the circumstances were completely different in Poland than they were in America. In Lodz my father and grandfather didn't have the benefit of history and probably weren't preparing in advance to flee, like they were in America. It is most likely that the coins weren't buried until they received the deportation notice and at that last moment they probably only had time to dig one location. Whatever the case may be, I don't have it in me to go back and re-dig the property. If a reader is willing to try, you have my blessing.

In March 2005, I was asked to speak about my quest at a Jewish community fundraising dinner in Windsor, Ontario. The speech was very well received and since then, I have been asked to speak at many other fundraisers. Although I have not been back to Poland since 2004, I continue to speak of my quest up until to this day. Every time I prepare to speak, I relive the journey many times over.

In October 2011, my mother fell and fractured her nose. Although her injuries were not severe, the nursing home staff panicked due to the amount of bleeding, which normally accompanies a broken nose, and had her rushed to the hospital. While she was hospitalized, dosing errors of pain medication and a misdiagnosis as to the extent of her injury led to her being unnecessarily and dangerously placed on a ventilator. Improper care and incorrect placement of the endotracheal tube resulted in a collapsed lung and severe pneumonia. My mother never recovered from these hospital-induced conditions and died in January 2012 at eighty-seven years old. It was a cruel twist of irony that the last physician to intervene on her behalf in a positive manner was the Nazi doctor nicknamed the "Angel of Death," Josef Mengele himself. He likely saved her life on that day in Auschwitz sixty-eight years earlier when he took her and her mother out of the line and sent them to work in his kitchen.

A little more than a year after my mother died, I decided to sell my horse farm and veterinary clinic and move to Laguna Beach, California. After several back and knee surgeries in the preceding couple of years, I was ready to retire from the horse business. Further incentive was provided when the Ontario Provincial Government made the questionable decision to discontinue a nearly one-billion-dollar funding agreement with the horse racing industry. This was a devastating blow and pretty much destroyed the business. In April 2014, after a year of trying, I was finally able to sell my farm and semi-retire to California.

Shortly after I had arrived in California, I arranged to do a speech at the Chabad Center in Laguna Beach on International Holocaust Remembrance Day. After seeing a flyer advertising the event, a former employee of my father's electrical business, now living in California, called me. He said that he had no idea of my father's complex history and was amazed to learn that my father was on Schindler's List. He added that my father actually had a list of his own. I then asked him what he meant by this. He responded that there were many struggling immigrants and troubled youths that were now successful electrical contractors because my father gave them a chance and a job and taught them the trade and how to run a business. But more importantly he taught them how to be a *mensch* (good and moral person), the former employee said. He then said that he loved my father and has enjoyed tremendous success because of opportunity my father gave him.

After I hung up the phone, the line from the Jewish Talmud that was used in the movie *Schindler's List* came to me: "He who saves a life, is considered as if he saved the world entire." It seems that my father remembered the act of kindness showed to him by Oscar Schindler and went on to contribute his part to make the world a better place. It is now my job to carry on his mission.

As for the coins, ultimately, I left them in Poland. I look at it this way: financially I don't need them at this point and by leaving them in the Lodz Museum, the Israelis are happy, the Poles are happy, and I look like a hero to them instead of a stereotypical money hungry Jew, like the one portrayed in the Anatevka restaurant lobby. From my perspective, although they are currently in a museum in Lodz, the coins are actually mine and are my investment in the Bank of Poland. In the fifteen years they've been there, gold has gone up 300 percent and the coin values have also tripled. Not a bad capital gains free return on my investment. Over the years since they've been discovered, I have thought about ways to successfully recover the coins, if and when that happens it will be featured in my next book. To be continued...

Index

CPSIA information can be obtained
at www.ICGtesting.com
Printed in the USA
BVHW040839120519
547972BV00001B/1/P

9 781644 690093